Evolutionary Explanations of Human Behaviour

In recent years, a new discipline has arisen that argues human behaviour can be understood in terms of evolutionary processes. *Evolutionary Explanations of Human Behaviour* is an introductory-level book covering evolutionary psychology, this new and controversial field. The book deals with three main areas: human reproductive behaviour, evolutionary explanations of mental disorders and the evolution of intelligence and the brain. The book is particularly suitable for the AQA-A A2 syllabus, but will also be of interest to undergraduates studying evolutionary psychology for the first time and anyone with a general interest in this new discipline.

John Cartwright is a senior lecturer in Biology at Chester College of Higher Education, an institution affiliated to the University of Liverpool. He teaches courses on evolution, evolutionary psychology as well as the history of science, and is the author of several books in these areas.

D0257146

Routledge Modular Psychology

Series editors: Cara Flanagan is a Reviser for AS and A2 level Psychology and lectures at Inverness College. Philip Banyard is Associate Senior Lecturer in Psychology at Nottingham Trent University and a Chief Examiner for AS and A2 level Psychology. Both are experienced writers.

The *Routledge Modular Psychology* series is a completely new approach to introductory-level psychology, tailor-made to the new modular style of teaching. Each short book covers a topic in more detail than any large textbook can, allowing teacher and student to select material exactly to suit any particular course or project.

The books have been written especially for those students new to higher-level study, whether at school, college or university. They include specially designed features to help with technique, such as a model essay at an average level with an examiner's comments to show how extra marks can be gained. The authors are all examiners and teachers at the introductory level.

The *Routledge Modular Psychology* texts are all user-friendly and accessible and include the following features:

- practice essays with specialist commentary to show how to achieve a higher grade
- chapter summaries to assist with revision
- progress and review exercises
- glossary of key terms
- summaries of key research
- further reading to stimulate ongoing study and research
- cross-referencing to other books in the series

Also available in this series (titles listed by syllabus section):

For Arthur and Dorothy

Evolutionary Explanations of Human Behaviour

John H. Cartwright

First published 2001
by Routledge
27 Church Road, Hove BN3 2FA

Simultaneously published in the USA and Canada
by Taylor & Francis Inc.
29 West 35th Street, New York NY 10001

Routledge is an imprint of the Taylor & Francis Group

© 2001 Psychology Press

Typeset in Times and Frutiger by Keystroke,
Jacaranda Lodge, Wolverhampton
Printed and bound in Great Britain
by TJ International Ltd, Padstow, Cornwall

Cover design by Terry Foley

British Library Cataloguing in Publication Data
A catalogue record for this book is available from the British Library

Library of Congress Cataloging-in-Publication Data
Cartwright, John, 1953–
    Evolutionary explanations of human behaviour / John H. Cartwright
        p. cm. — (Routledge modular psychology)
    Includes bibliographical references and index.
    ISBN 0-415-24147-2 — ISBN 0-415-24148-0 (pbk.)
1. Behavior evolution. 2. Genetic psychology. I. Title. II. Series.
BF701 .C375 2001
155.7—dc21   2001031917

ISBN 0–415–24147–2 (hbk)
ISBN 0–415–24148–0 (pbk)

Contents

List of illustrations   xi

1 Introduction   **1**
Psychology and the theory of evolution   1
The mechanism of Darwinian evolution by
    natural selection   2
The nature of evolutionary adaptations   5
Why apples are sweet: ultimate and proximate
    explanations in psychology   7
Case study: The avoidance of incest   9
Summary   12

2 Sexual reproduction   **15**
The sexual imperative: sperm meets egg   15
The terminology of mating behaviour: systems and
    strategies   16
Patterns of human mating   18
    Contemporary traditional or pre-industrial societies   19
    Hunter-gathering societies   21
    Despots in early civilizations   22
    The female perspective   23
Summary   25

3 Sexual selection 27
Natural selection and sexual selection compared 27
Inter- and intrasexual selection 29
Parental investment 30
Potential reproduction rates: humans and other animals 31
The operational sex ratio 33
Consequences of sexual selection 36
  Sexual dimorphism in body size 37
  Sexual enthusiasm 39
  *Post-copulatory intrasexual competition: sperm
    competition* 40
  Good genes and honest signals 42
Summary 47

4 Unravelling human sexuality 49
Comparisons between humans and other primates 49
  Differences in body size between males and females 49
  Testis size 50
  *Testis size and bodily dimorphism applied
    to humans* 51
Evolution and sexual desire: some expectations and
  approaches 56
  Cross-cultural comparisons using questionnaires 57
  Surveys using published advertisements 59
Facial attractiveness 62
Sexual jealousy 64
Summary 70

5 Archetypes of the psyche: fears and anxieties
as adaptive responses 73
The universality of emotional life 73
Mental health and archetypes of the psyche 75
Fears, anxieties and phobias 76
Summary 81

6 Evolutionary explanations of mental disorders 85
Mental disorders: problems of terminology 85
Mental abnormalities: some hypotheses 88
  Malfunctioning mental modules 88

Exiles from Eden   88
The adaptive conservatism hypothesis   94
Preparedness theory   95
The normal distribution theory   99
Social homeostasis or rank theories of depression   100
Ontogenetic or developmental theories   100
Inclusive fitness theories   102
A genetic basis for mental disorders   104
Unipolar and bipolar depression   105
Schizophrenia   105
The adaptive value of genetically based disorders   109
Evolutionary psychiatry: prospects   113
Summary   114

7 The evolution of brain size   **119**
The place of humans in nature   119
The importance of size   120
Brain size and the risks of childbirth   123
Brain size and mating behaviour   124
Brain size and scaling effects (allometry): a mathematical
   diversion   125
Ancestral brains   127
Summary   131

8 The evolution of intelligence   **133**
Origins of primate intelligence   133
Environmental factors: foraging behaviour and
   private intelligence   134
Social factors: machiavellian intelligence and the
   theory of mind   134
Food or sociality: testing the theories   136
Methodological problems   136
Brain size and primate diet   138
Intelligence and the neocortex   139
Environmental and social complexity and neocortex
   volume   140
Problems with foraging and machiavellian theories   142
Other theories of the evolution of intelligence   143

*Sexual selection and the evolution of the brain:
the display hypothesis*   144
*Hardware–software co-evolution: the stimulus of
language*   145
Tool use   146
Summary   150

9 Study aids   **153**
Improving your essay writing skills   153
Practice essay 1   155
Practice essay 2   159
Practice essay 3   162

Key Research Summaries   166
Glossary   169
Answers to progress exercises   175
Bibliography   185
Index   193

Illustrations

Figures

1.1 A Darwinian wheel of life   4
1.2 Photograph of Charles Darwin by Ernest Edwards,
     taken in about 1870   5
2.1 Human mating systems in traditional cultures prior
     to Western influences   20
3.1 Sexual selection as found in the hummingbird species
     Sparthura underwoodi   29
3.2 Intrasexual competition and the operational sex ratio   34
3.3 Detail from *The Rake's Progress* by William Hogarth   36
3.4 Sexual dimorphism in the beetle species *Chasognathus
     grantii*   38
4.1 Body size dimorphism against mating system   50
4.2 An adult male chimpanzee (*Pan troglodytes*)   51
4.3 Relative testis size against mating system   52
4.4 Female's view of males illustrating relative size of body,
     penis and testes.   54
4.5 Typical 'lonely hearts' advertisement   60
4.6 Percentage of advertisers seeking and offering
     physical appearance and financial security according
     to gender   61
4.7 Percentage of advertisers in personal columns seeking
     resources   62

4.8 Total number of divorces in England and Wales in 1995   67

4.9 Percentage of divorces in each age group according to sex and age group for England and Wales, 1995   68

4.10 Percentage of divorces as a result of adultery by sex in each age group   69

5.1 *The Scream* from a lithograph by Edvard Munch (1863–1944) made in 1895   78

5.2 *Anxiety* by Munch (1896)   81

6.1 A hypothetical normal distribution of the anxiety response   99

7.1 Traditional taxonomy of the human species   120

7.2 Time chart of some early hominids   121

7.3 Growth of brain size in relation to body size for mammals   126

7.4 Logarithmic plot of brain size against body size   127

7.5 Growth in human brain volume during human evolution   128

7.6 Evolutionary tree of selected primates   130

8.1 Triune model of the brain as proposed by MacLean   140

8.2 Plot of group size against neocortex ratio for various species of primates   141

8.3 Relationship between neocortical ratio and index of tactical deception for a variety of primates   142

8.4 Some possible evolutionary stimuli on the growth of hominid brains   149

Tables

2.1 Simple classification of mating systems   17

2.2 Four basic mating systems   18

3.1 Mechanisms of intersexual competition   44

4.1 Physical characteristics of the great apes in relation to mating and reproduction   53

4.2 Predictions on mate choice preferences tested cross-culturally by Buss (1989)   58

4.3 Number of cultures supporting or otherwise hypotheses on gender differences in mate preference   59

4.4	Predicted differences in the experience of jealousy by men and women	65
5.1	Types of fear and their adaptive origins	79
6.1	Leading causes of world DALYs, 1990	94
6.2	Selection of results of an epidemiological study of phobias on a sample of 20,000 American subjects	98
6.3	Probability of developing schizophrenia	106
6.4	Approximate risk ratios for various disorders	108
7.1	Body weights, brain weights and encephalisation quotients for selected apes and hominids	129
8.1	Comparison of brain sizes of howler and spider monkeys	138

Introduction

◈ Psychology and the theory of evolution
◈ The mechanism of Darwinian evolution by natural selection
◈ The nature of evolutionary adaptations
◈ Why apples are sweet: ultimate and proximate explanations
   in psychology
◈ Case study: the avoidance of incest
◈ Summary

Psychology and the theory of evolution

When Darwin published his *Origin of Species* in 1859, he was confident that in time it would supply a new basis for all the life sciences. Towards the end of the *Origin* he wrote:

> In the distant future I see open fields for far more important researches. Psychology will be based on a new foundation, that of the necessary acquirement of each mental power and capacity by gradation. Light will be thrown on the origin of man and his history. (Darwin, 1859, p. 458)

Darwin was perhaps overoptimistic, for despite some early work by William James in America it was not until the 1970s that the evolutionary approach to human behaviour in the form of sociobiology and what was to become evolutionary psychology took root. For much of the twentieth century psychologists failed to follow Darwin's lead and either ignored or misinterpreted Darwin. Many psychologists and biologists, and I count myself one of them, now think that it is time for psychology once again to re-establish links with the central **paradigm** that underlies all of the life sciences: the theory of evolution by natural selection. I will leave it up to you, the student, to read this book and decide if you think psychology has anything to learn from Darwinism.

The mechanism of Darwinian evolution by natural selection

The American philosopher of science, Daniel Dennett, once said that 'If I were to give an award for the best idea anyone has ever had, I'd give it to Darwin, ahead of Newton and Einstein and everyone else' (Dennett, 1995). As we grasp the awesome significance of Darwinian ideas it is hard not to share Dennett's enthusiasm. In the theory of evolution we have a theory as to where life came from, why life exists at all and how the construction and behaviour of organisms serve their survival.

The essential features of Darwinism can be summarised as a series of statements about the characteristics of living things:

1. Based on such characteristics as anatomy, physiology and behaviour, individual animals can be grouped into **species**. A species is not entirely an artificial construct since members of the same species, if they reproduce sexually, can, by definition, breed with each other to produce fertile offspring. Using this criterion, for example, all humans belong to the same species: *Homo sapiens*.
2. Within a given species or population variation exists; individuals are not identical and differ in physical and behavioural characteristics.
3. Many physical and behavioural traits are expressions of information to be found in the **genome** of individuals. The genome consists of strands of **DNA** carrying information in the form of a molecular code. Individuals inherit their DNA from their parents (50% from each) and pass their own DNA on to their offspring.
4. In sexually reproducing species, such as humans, offspring are not identical to their parents. This is because each new individual

contains a whole mixture of genes from each parent in a new combination. Some of these genes may not even have been switched on in our parents. Apart from rare cases of identical twins, we are all genetically unique. In addition, variation is enriched by the occurrence of spontaneous but random novelty. Genes often suffer damage or **mutations** and a feature may appear that was not present in previous generations or present to a different degree. Most mutations are harmful and all animals have chemical screening techniques to root them out. Occasionally, however, such changes may bring about some benefit.

5. Resources required by organisms to thrive and reproduce are limited. Competition must inevitably arise and some organisms will leave fewer offspring than others will.

6. Some variations will confer an advantage on their possessors in terms of access to these resources and hence in terms of leaving offspring.

7. Those variants that leave more offspring will tend to be preserved and gradually increase in frequency in the population. If the departure from the original ancestor is sufficiently radical, new species may form and natural selection will have brought about evolutionary change.

8. As a consequence of natural selection, organisms will eventually become adapted to their environments and their mode of life in the broad sense of being well suited to the essential processes of life, such as obtaining food, avoiding predation, finding mates, competing with rivals for limited resources and so on. Organisms, through this process of **adaptation**, will look as if they were expertly designed for their activities.

To this we may now add specific expectations about the human body and mind:

9. Because of Darwinian evolution, both the human body and the mind can be expected to be structured in ways that helped our ancestors to survive and reproduce. Since hominids have been on the planet for about 5 million years the human body and mind should, by now, be well adapted for these purposes. Consequently, human behaviour, at least to the degree that it is under genetic influence, will be geared towards survival and ultimately reproductive success.

These ideas can be described schematically as a sort of cycle involving the birth and death of organisms, a Darwinian wheel of life (Figure 1.1).

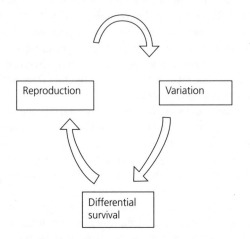

Figure 1.1 **A Darwinian wheel of life. The birth and death of thousands of individual organisms result in gradual modification through differential survival. The result is the gradual formation of new species and, crucially for Darwinian psychology, the emergence of adaptations**

In applying Darwinism to human behaviour, it is important to distinguish between **genotype** and **phenotype**. Your genotype consists of the set of genes that you inherited from your mother and father. Such genes contain the information needed by cells to carry out their functions of growth and reproduction. The information stored there, in concert with environmental influences when you were growing and those acting now, determines who you are. The finished product, yourself, is the phenotype. It is important to realise that the flow of information from the genes to the phenotype is one way. Your genes can influence your development, behaviour and personality, but you cannot alter the information stored in your genes. If, for example, you spend years of study learning Chinese, your offspring will not speak Chinese, nor, sadly, will they necessarily find it easier than you to learn Chinese. This is sometimes expressed abstractly in the rule that acquired characteristics cannot be inherited. The environment in which an animal grows can influence the phenotype but not the messages found along its genes.

The nature of evolutionary adaptations

Movement around the Darwinian wheel of life (Figure 1.1) will result in organisms that are adapted to maximise their **reproductive fitness**. Fitness here refers to the special biological sense of being capable of leaving offspring. Organisms will behave so as to ensure that they reproduce successfully in competition with others. There is no special virtue or purpose in this; it is simply that organisms that, perhaps through chance genetic variation, were less skilled or earnest in this process have died out. It is a truism but worth repeating that none of us is descended from an infertile ancestor.

Figure 1.2 Photograph of Charles Darwin by Ernest Edwards, taken in about 1870

An important question to address when studying the evolution of human behaviour is the problem of whether behaviour will appear to be adapted to current conditions or to conditions in the past. A behavioural **trait** that we study now may have been shaped for some adaptive purpose long ago. The environment may have changed so that the **adaptive significance** of the trait under study is now not at all obvious; indeed, it may now even appear maladaptive. When human babies are born they have a strong clutching instinct and will grab fingers and other objects with remarkable strength. This may be a leftover from when to grab a mother's fur helped reduce accidents from falling. It is not clear that it helps the newborn in contemporary culture.

The problem applies to other animals as well of course. When a hedgehog rolls up into a ball in the face of oncoming traffic this is no longer a sensible response to the threat from a predator. The problem is especially acute for humans, however, since over the last 10,000 years we have radically transformed the environment in which we live. We now daily encounter situations and challenges that were simply absent during the period when the human genome was moulded into its present form. It could be expected that we have adaptations for running, fighting, throwing things, weighing up rivals, securing alliances, finding and seducing mates, and making babies but not specifically for reading, driving cars, playing tennis, studying psychology or coping with jet-lag. Logically, any **adaptation** that we have now must have been shaped by the past. One crucial question therefore is whether the human psyche was designed specifically to cope with problems found in the **environment of our evolutionary adaptation** (EEA) – usually taken to be between 2 million and 40,000 years before the present – or whether our psyche is flexible enough to direct behaviours that still tend to increase our reproductive fitness in the contemporary world.

As an illustrative example, consider food preferences. Humans, and especially children, are strongly attracted to salty and fatty foods high in calories and sugars. Our taste buds were probably finely and appropriately adjusted for the Old Stone Age (roughly 200,000 to 10,000 years before the present) when such foods were in short supply and to receive a lot of pleasure from their consumption was a useful way to motivate us to search out more. Such tastes are now far from adaptive in an environment in developed countries where fast food high in salt, fat and processed carbohydrates can be bought cheaply, with deleterious health consequences such as arteriosclerosis and tooth decay.

There is obviously some truth in this viewpoint, but it is also important to note that natural selection can shape how development and learning occur in relation to local environments. It follows that behaviour does not have to be forced into the category of 'hard-wired' mental tools designed for an ancient environment. Natural selection could have shaped our minds to behave in ways that increase our **fitness** under contemporary conditions. Symons (1992) criticised this latter approach, however, by remarking that if modern males really did behave so as to maximise fitness then 'opportunities to make deposits in sperm banks would be immensely competitive . . . with the possibility of reverse embezzlement by male sperm bank officers an ever-present problem' (p. 155).

The answer of course is that natural selection did not provide us with a vague fitness-increasing drive. The genes made sure that fitness maximisation was an unconscious urge – an urge that certainly must have predated consciousness. Like the heartbeat, it was too valuable to be placed under conscious control. Instead, males and females were provided with powerful sexual drives. Counting the size of the queue outside a sperm bank would be a fruitless way of assessing whether males pursue fitness-maximising strategies. Counting partners and real sexual opportunities, however, might be better. If sperm banks were set up to allow males to deposit sperm more naturally (in other words, through sexual intercourse) the queues would probably be longer.

Why apples are sweet: ultimate and proximate explanations in psychology

Consider the question 'Why are apples sweet?' and the type of answers we can give. A biochemist might reply that it is due to the shape of the sugar molecules of fructose and sucrose triggering a response on a taste bud receptor on the tongue. A neurobiologist (someone who studies the brain from a chemical and biochemical point of view) might complement this by locating the nerve pathways and the part of the brain that is activated when the sweet sensation is experienced. Both explanations are partial and fail to explain, for example, why humans find apples sweet but many other animals (such as cats) probably do not. What both the biochemist and the neurobiologist have done is to provide **proximate** explanations or to reveal proximate mechanisms. In this context proximate means near to or immediate. The proximate cause of a heart attack, for example, may be reduced blood flow to the muscles of the heart. The ultimate cause may be poor diet, or stress or some genetic defect at birth. For the **ultimate** explanation of sweetness – sometimes called, rather confusingly for the student, **functional** – we need to dig deeper and call upon Darwinian psychology. The Darwinian or ultimate explanation would run something like this. Humans experience a sweet and pleasurable sensation on tasting apples because apples contain essential nutrients such as minerals and vitamin C. The pleasure experienced on eating provided the motivational stimulus for our remote ancestors to eat such foodstuffs; our ancestors that were disposed in this way to consume apples and other fruits thrived, whereas those that failed to consume them died out. The argument probably sounds a little pedantic but it is essential to grasp the logic of natural and sexual selection. We can now see why cats are not too fond of apples. Cats can manufacture their own vitamin C and consequently there is no real advantage to them in consuming fruit.

It is important to grasp that the genes that shape our taste bud circuits and other neural pathways are not striving to survive by ensuring that we obtain our essential nutrients; it is simply that those that dispose us to behave in certain ways do survive and others are lost, but the whole show is not going anywhere. We must also be wary of interpreting the word mechanism. In evolutionary psychology, the word mechanism is used as a shorthand for the series of neural circuits, mental dispositions and so on that promote certain types of behaviour. We should not think, however, that behaviour is simply mechanistic or that it is invariant and 'hard-wired'. Hard-wiring may be suitable for ants but evolution gave up hard-wiring the higher mammals long ago. Our lives are too complex and we need to learn so much from experience that fixed patterns of behaviour would be unsuitable for us and unable to solve our survival problems. We need to weigh up evidence, evaluate alternatives and plan courses of action and all this requires some cognitive subtlety. Nevertheless, evolution has crafted our brains around the biological imperatives of survival and reproduction; we are inclined to make certain types of decisions, to find certain foods or people attractive. Despite our mental sophistication there are still those 'murmurings within' (to use a phrase of the American evolutionist David Barash) that structure our actions, behaviour and thoughts.

One awesome implication of Darwinism, that many find difficult to stomach, is that there is no ultimate purpose, design or destiny to the natural world. Natural selection is not driving life to any particular end or goal, although it is capable of producing intelligent beings such as ourselves who can worry about this.

Case study: the avoidance of incest

One of the best and clearest illustrations of the difference between proximate and functional (ultimate) explanations arises from the **Westermarck effect**, a mechanism that offers an explanation for the avoidance of incest. In virtually all societies incest is frowned upon or declared illegal. Very few men have sex with their sisters or mothers. Sexual abuse of daughters by fathers is more common but still relatively rare compared to heterosexual sex between unrelated individuals. We can consider two explanations of these facts. One is that related individuals secretly desire incest but that culture imposes strict taboos to prevent its occurrence. The other is that humans possess some inherited mechanism that causes them not to find close relatives sexually attractive.

The first of these explanations came from Sigmund Freud. Freud's theory suggested that people have inherent incestuous desires; they are not observed in action very often partly because they are 'repressed' and partly because society has (presumably for the benefit of the health of its members) imposed strict taboos. Suggesting that incestuous urges are repressed, and so difficult to observe, makes it difficult of course to refute the idea that we have them in the first place. A further difficulty is that Freud is essentially suggesting that evolution has not only failed to generate a mechanism to suppress incest, which as we will see below is positively harmful to the health of any offspring produced, but somehow has led to a positive preference for it.

An alternative theory was proposed by the Finnish anthropologist Edward Westermarck in 1891. To understand the logic of Westermarck's argument some insights from twentieth-century genetics are useful. Humans who mate with a close relative have a high chance of producing offspring that inherit genetic abnormalities. The reason is that all of us carry a pair of genes for any given trait: one inherited from our mother and one from our father. All of us also carry a few faulty genes. About one in 25 Caucasians, for example, carry a faulty version (sometimes referred to as the 'recessive **allele**') of a gene that, if expressed, leads to the condition of **cystic fibrosis**. Fortunately, the vast majority of those that do carry the gene also carry a normal (dominant) version as the other one of the pair and so cystic fibrosis is a rare condition. Simple probability tells us, however, that the chance of two cystic fibrosis carriers meeting is $1/25 \times 1/25$, which gives one in 625. If such couples do mate then each offspring has a one in four chance of inheriting both defective alleles and hence developing cystic fibrosis. This does happen of course and one in 2500 ($1/625 \times \frac{1}{4}$) Caucasian children are born with cystic fibrosis.

It might be supposed that natural selection should have eliminated cystic fibrosis by now but a simple calculation shows that if carriers (not sufferers) have just a 2.3% advantage over non-carriers then the deleterious gene will persist in the gene pool indefinitely (see also the section on 'The adaptive value of genetically based disorders' in Chapter 6).

Now consider for a moment two children, one boy and one girl, of parents that, unknown to themselves, are carriers of the cystic fibrosis gene. Each child has a ¼ chance of inheriting two copies of the recessive allele from their parents, and falling victim to cystic fibrosis; a ¼ chance of inheriting two good alleles and growing up normally; and a ½ chance of becoming a **carrier** like their parents. We will take the most likely option and assume that both the brother and sister are carriers. If the boy and his sister were to find each other sexually attractive, mate and have children, then the chance of each of their children developing cystic fibrosis is once again one in four. This in itself is an enormously high risk. Cystic fibrosis is just one of many genetic faults: it is estimated that every one of us carries between three and five recessive alleles that if we had both copies would prove lethal. In short, modern genetics explains why mating behaviour between close relatives is bad news for any offspring.

If you have a brother or sister you almost certainly will find the idea of mating with them repellent and preposterous, but it is the source of this very feeling we need to explain. This is where the argument of Westermarck comes to the fore. We can see that mating with members of the opposite sex that carry the same recessive alleles as you is, genetically speaking, inviting trouble, but it is difficult to tell if they do have such genes. We know, however, that siblings are much more likely to carry such defects than complete strangers – simply because most genetic defects are inherited from our parents. Westermarck suggested that siblings do not mate with each other because during their childhood development they become disposed not to find them sexually attractive. Westermarck argued that humans use a simple (unconscious) rule for deciding if another individual is related or not. If humans avoid mating with individuals they have been reared with during childhood then there is a good chance they will also avoid mating with close relatives. Freud was inclined to reject Westermarck's hypothesis, which he regarded as absurd, since it flew in the face of his Oedipus complex – something that Freud saw as core to his whole psychoanalytical framework.

Evidence in favour of Westermarck's hypothesis comes from Israeli kibbutzim, where unrelated children are reared together in crèches. This often results in close friendships but marriages between kibbutz children are rare (Parker, 1976). Further support for the effect comes from a study on 'minor marriages' or *sim-pua* in Taiwan by Arthur Wolf of Stanford University. Minor marriages occur when a genetically unrelated infant girl is adopted by a family and raised with the biological sons in the family. The motive seems to be to ensure that a son finds a partner since eventually the girl is married to a son. Wolf studied the histories of thousands of Taiwanese women and found their experiences to favour the Westermarck hypothesis. Compared to other arranged marriages, minor marriages were much more likely to fail: the women usually resisted the marriage, the divorce rate was three times other marriages, couples produced 40% fewer children and extramarital affairs were more common.

More recent evidence in favour of the Westermarck effect comes from the work of Bevc and Silverman (2000). These authors found that siblings who were reared together were much less likely to engage in genital sexual activity than siblings who were separated in infancy and reared apart.

The Westermarck effect is an instructive illustration of the relationship between genes and environment. The instruction to avoid sex with others who shared your childhood is a disposition that we are directed to follow by the way genes have structured our brains. The target group of individuals to whom this applies is socially determined. The ultimate explanation of the incest taboo resides in the need to avoid **inbreeding**; the proximate mechanism is to develop in such a way as not to find members of the opposite sex you grew up with sexually attractive.

The need to avoid excessive inbreeding also applies to non-human animals of course. Many species have a far simpler mechanism to achieve this, such as parents forcing the infants to disperse from their home area as they approach maturity. The chances of any individual then meeting up with a relative are reduced.

Progress exercise

Bad smells

Why do some things smell bad? Think of a few cases where the smell of some objects is repellent. Offer a proximate explanation (in general terms) why the smell is perceived as bad; then offer an ultimate explanation.

Summary

- Evolution occurs through the differential reproductive success of genes. Genes that prescribe characteristics that help the host to produce more offspring than other genes will be preferentially selected. Change occurs because genes are periodically modified by spontaneous mutations. Good genes win through while bad genes die out. The net result, after many generations of this sifting and sorting, is that animals will come to be well adapted to their environments and to the imperatives of finding mates and leaving new offspring. The implication of this process for psychology is that the human mind will have been shaped by natural selection. Consequently, we can expect many aspects of our psychology to reflect the adaptations that natural selection has given us.
- To understand the mechanism of natural selection we need to distinguish between genotype and phenotype. The genotype consists of the genes that carry the information needed to build organisms. The phenotype is the result of the interaction between genes and the environment within an individual. Whereas environmental factors may strongly influence the way genes are expressed within an organism, the outcome of this interaction cannot be communicated to the genotype. Characteristics acquired in the lifetime of an individual are thus not inherited by offspring.

- An important distinction exists between proximate and ultimate explanations for human behaviour. Proximate explanations explain behaviour in terms of neural pathways, biochemical reactions, hormonal mechanisms, brain structures and social conditioning. However, essential as they are, proximate explanations do not address the fundamental question of why humans are built in this way. Ultimate explanations point to the adaptive or functional significance of behaviour and dispositions in terms of how such mechanisms conferred survival advantages on our ancestors. Darwinian psychology seeks to provide ultimate explanations for the way humans behave.

Place the terms given into their correct position in the table.

Terms: *ultimate explanation, adaptation, species, natural selection, phenotype, genotype, DNA, genotype, proximate explanation, mutation*

Description/definition	Term
An account of the cause of something in terms of mechanisms that have developed in the lifetime of an individual, e.g. nervous structures, hormonal effects	
The sum of the information carried on the genes of an individual	
The process of selecting out successful genes and allowing unsuccessful ones to become rare or extinct	
A group of similar-looking organisms that can interbreed to produce fertile offspring	

Review exercise

Description/definition	Term
A sudden and undirected change in the molecular structure of DNA	
The body of an organism as a result of both environmental and genetic effects	
An explanation of some feature of the human mind or body that refers to the way such a feature helped ancestors survive	
The process by which organisms evolve to be well suited to their mode of life	
A long spiral molecule that carries the information necessary to build cells and bodies	

Further reading

Buss, D. (1999). *Evolutionary Psychology*. Needham Heights, MA: Allyn & Bacon. See Chapter 1. A textbook designed for American undergraduates but parts are relevant to this topic and accessible to the good A-level student.

2

Sexual reproduction

The sexual imperative: sperm meets egg
The terminology of mating behaviour: systems and strategies
Patterns of human mating
Summary

The sexual imperative: sperm meets egg

Some organisms, such as starfish, bacteria and many plant species, are capable of producing asexually; that is, they do not require a sexual partner. The population consists of females that simply produce copies of themselves – so-called clones. Humans are not like this and from an evolutionary perspective it is imperative that individuals of sexually reproducing species like ourselves find a mate. It is through mating that genes (the 'immortal replicators' to use Dawkins' phrase) secure their passage to the next generation. It is hardly surprising then that sex is an enormously powerful driving force in the lives of humans and is attended to with a sometimes irrational and desperate urgency. In its most elemental form, sex consists of the fusion of two **gametes**: one from the male (the **sperm**) and one from the female (the **ovum**).

Although the first sexually reproducing organisms probably produced gametes from males or females of equal size, for most species alive today the size of gametes from males and females is vastly different. In the case of humans, for example, the ovum is about 0.1 mm in diameter, while the head of the sperm from the male only measures about 0.005 mm. Right at the outset then we can see that males and females have plumped for different sexual strategies. Males produce large quantities of small, highly mobile sperm that seek out the much larger gamete supplied by the female. The female invests far more energy per gamete than does the male. But there are other differences in investment and behaviour that also have a bearing on the sexual behaviour of males and females, and this unequal investment is but a first step in a tangled game of biological sexual politics. To study the mating behaviour of humans more fully we now need to introduce some basic terminology.

The terminology of mating behaviour: systems and strategies

Older biology textbooks will often associate a species with a particular mating system and, although this approach is outdated, the terminology is still useful. A simple classification of some common mating systems is shown in Table 2.1.

So where do we place humans in Table 2.1? This is an extremely difficult question to answer. Part of the problem is that humans are very variable and you can probably think of cases that fall into every one of the categories above. Nevertheless, it is still valid to ask what type of behaviour best characterises human males and females. The law in Western countries prescribes monogamy but this may not be the ancestral system to which we are adapted. Indeed the high failure rate of many marriages and the frequency in which adultery is cited as grounds for divorce suggest that we are not naturally disposed to be 100% monogamous. However, there are deeper problems to tackle before we can answer this question. In attempting to ascribe mating systems to particular species, we are overlooking several facts:

- In the case of **polygyny**, males and females are behaving differently although they are of the same species. In the case of elephant seals, for example, males are highly polygynous and successful ones may mate with dozens of females in a season, whereas females are monogamous and mate with only one.
- Species in themselves do not behave as a single entity; it is the behaviour of individuals that is the raw material for evolution.

Table 2.1 Simple classification of mating systems

System	Mating exclusivity and/or pair bond character
MONOGAMY	**Copulation with only one partner**
Annual	**Pair bond re-formed between different individuals each year**
Perennial	**Pair bond formed for life**
POLYGAMY	**One sex copulates with more than one member of the other sex**
Polygyny	**Where a male mates with several females. Females with only one male**
Successive	**Males bond with several females in breeding system but only one at a time**
Simultaneous	**Males bond with several females simultaneously**
Polyandry	**One female mates with several males. Males with only one female**
Successive	**Females bond with several males but one at a time**
Simultaneous	**Females bond with several males at the same time**

Natural selection can only act upon individuals, ruthlessly exterminating those that are unsuccessful and allowing those that are better adapted to pass their genes to the next generation. To understand behaviour we need to consider how that behaviour helps or retards the chances of individuals reproducing.

- Within any species individuals even of one sex may differ and utilise different strategies. Where there is a genetic basis to this, it is sometimes known as a polymorphism (lit.: many shaped). Humans are polymorphic for a number of characteristics, such as blood groups or presence or absence of freckles. Hence in the **gene pool** of a species there may be genes that predispose some individuals more towards monogamy and others towards polygyny.

In biology and Darwinian psychology it is now recognised that a better approach is to focus on strategies pursued by individuals in their attempt to improve their reproductive prospects within the conditions that prevail at any one time. The most common behaviour of individuals in any species may then allow us to loosely apply the label of a 'mating system' as a matter of descriptive convenience.

Some animal behaviourists prefer to describe the social arrangement that facilitates mating in terms of the number and sex of the individuals. Table 2.2 shows how this works. Hence we would say that the mating behaviour of gorillas is uni-male, multi-female, since they live in polygynous groups where one male has access to a 'harem of females'. The mating behaviour of chimps would be described as multi-male, multi-female, since they live in mixed groups where both males and females may have several sexual partners.

Table 2.2 Four basic mating systems		
	Uni-male	*Multi-female*
Uni-female	**Monogamy**	**Polyandry**
Multi-female	**Polygyny**	**Promiscuity/ polygynandry**

Patterns of human mating

In a story by William James a character called Mrs Amos Pinchot writes down a piece of short verse following a dream:

Hogamus, higamous
Man is polygamous
Higamus, hogamus
Woman monogamous

Nonsensical, sexist or basically correct? What strategies might human males and females be expected to pursue? To address this question we could start by making some simple predictions from the basic biological differences between men and women. Humans, as mammals, are live-bearing and consequently offspring must be nourished before birth. This is done by a placental food delivery system. Once the young are born, nurture is then given by female lactation. It follows that females make a huge investment in parenting, a good part of which cannot be supplied by the male. If the mammalian male is to increase his reproductive success, his best strategy would be to divert more effort into mating than to parenting; in other words, to pursue polygyny. A female will be more disposed towards **monogamy** (or monandry: having only one male partner) since the bottleneck to her reproductive success is not the number of impregnations she can solicit but the resources she is able to accumulate for gestation and nurture. As a first-order approximation then it might be expected that men are inclined to behave polygynously whereas women should be more monogamous. It turns out that this is an oversimplification and will need to be refined later but it is worth pausing for a moment and examining the evidence. How would we test this prediction? The problem with simply issuing questionnaires or looking at sexual practices around us is that Western cultures have been strongly influenced by Judaeo-Christianity, with its firm stance on the requirement for monogamy. In addition, polygyny, where one man has many wives, is largely outlawed in the West. Looking at modern cultures therefore we might only observe a suppression rather than an expression of natural or innate drives. With this in mind, it might be more useful to examine people pursuing a more traditional mode of life or people living in pre Christian cultures.

Contemporary traditional or pre-industrial societies

Humans living in today's industrial or more developed countries are living under conditions very different from those that existed where the basic plan of the human genome was laid down. Nearly all the genes that you and I now carry around in our cells, including those that inform our sexual inclinations, were present in our ancestors 40,000 years ago living in the Old Stone Age. So if we want to ascertain the sexual behaviour of humans before our habits were transformed by industrialisation, or before our heads were filled with strict religious and political codes of conduct, it makes sense to look at cultures still existing that are likely to contain vestiges of an earlier mode of living. Alternatively, we could look at cultures that have been relatively isolated from Western influence and maintain traditional patterns of life. Figure 2.1 shows the pattern of mating systems observed in such cultures.

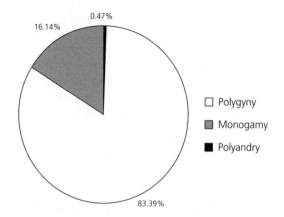

Figure 2.1 **Human mating systems in traditional cultures prior to Western influences. Figure adapted from 'Human sperm competition' in *Sperm Competition and the Evolution of Animal Mating Systems* by R.L. Smith, copyright © 1984 by Academic Press, reproduced by permission of the publisher**

From Figure 2.1 it begins to look as if polygyny is quite common. It is difficult to arrive at totally reliable conclusions from such data, however, due to the problem of deciding how to count the data points. If we identify two cultures that practice, say, polygyny it could quantitatively represent two data points or one. It would count as two if the cultures were isolated and underwent independent social evolution but only one if they both descended from some ancestral culture that practised polygyny. In addition, the label polygyny may conceal a wider diversity of mating behaviour within the group, tribe or population. Even in polygynous societies, simple logic shows that not all men can be polygynous – there are not enough women to go round. It is often the case that in societies classified as polygynous only a small percentage of the men practise it. Nevertheless, the survey presented in Figure 2.1 does suggest that monogamy, so often held up as an ideal, may not be so common on a global scale.

Hunter-gathering societies

We have already noted that for most of our time on this planet we have lived in a hunter-gatherer lifestyle and it is reasonable to suppose that there are at least some similarities in the problems faced by contemporary hunter-gatherers to those dealt with by our ancestors 100,000 years ago.

Hunter-gatherers are people who have not domesticated plants or animals and so live a lifestyle that entails obtaining whatever food happens to be available in that locality. Studies show that food supply and the capture of meat through hunting are important factors in understanding the mating strategies of hunter-gatherers. Studies by Hill and Kaplan (1988) on the Ache people of Paraguay showed that men would often donate meat to women in exchange for sex. Studies on the !Kung San people of Botswana and the Yanomamo Indians of Venezuala also tend to reveal a pattern of mild polygyny (Chagnon, 1968).

As a general rule, however, it is very likely that a hunter-gathering way of life never really supported an extreme degree of polygyny. There are at least two reasons for this. The first is that hunting large animals is risky and needs a combination of cooperation and luck. Hunting is carried out by males (for the simple reason that human infants need a prolonged period of gestation and nurturing) and the cooperation needed for this means that male rivalry must be kept within strict limits. Following a kill, the meat must be shared between all those that helped, and indeed with other unsuccessful groups. This latter sharing makes good genetic sense. If a family cannot eat all the meat they have captured then it pays them to share with others in the expectation that they will receive return favours when they are unlucky. If a high degree of polygyny prevailed in such groups, the sexual rivalry would militate against this altruistic behaviour. It is significant that

21

the equitable sharing of hunted food is characteristic of hunter-gatherers and totally unlike other social hunting species where after a kill there is a free-for-all.

The second reason why extreme polygyny is unlikely to have been found among our hunter-gatherer ancestors is that meat is difficult to store. It is difficult to conceive how in a foraging culture sufficient wealth or resources could ever be accumulated by one man to support a sizeable harem. Predictably, in very few known hunter-gathering societies has a high level of polygyny been found. In most hunter-gathering groups men will have one or at most two wives. These are reasonable arguments but not cast-iron ones. One serious problem is that today's hunter-gatherers occupy areas of land that may not have been typical of the past. Much of the fertile and productive land has been developed by modern humans and contemporary hunter-gatherers may now face different, possibly more difficult, ecological conditions.

Despots in early civilisations

An examination of early historical societies allows us to observe how people have behaved under different cultural constraints and opportunities. The term historical societies usually refers to human groups living after the invention of agriculture (about 10,000 years ago) and when written records became available for the first time.

In the USA, Mildred Dickemann, John Hartung and Laura Betzig have all pioneered the Darwinian approach to human history. Betzig (1982, 1986) examined six civilisations of early history: Babylon, Egypt, India, China, the Incas and the Aztecs. She found that in all of them the accumulation of power and wealth by a ruling male elite was used to support a retinue of concubines for the exclusive pleasure of the ruler. The harems of these male rulers, often numbering hundreds or even thousands of concubines, were vigorously defended and guarded by eunuchs, with extreme penalties meted out to any subject who had sexual relations with the ruler's concubines.

In seeking to explain this phenomenon, it could be argued that such harems were displays of wealth – items of conspicuous consumption – or one of the many trappings of wealth and power that gave pleasure to the ruler. Each of these reasons may offer a partial explanation, but several features of the regulation of the harems do not fit easily into such conventional accounts. Betzig shows how the structure of the harem seems to be designed to ensure the maximum fertility of the women concerned as well as ensuring absolute confidence of paternity for the despot. The breast-feeding of infants helps illustrate this. While a woman is breast-feeding a child she ceases to ovulate; this in itself is a good evolutionary mechanism to ensure that a woman is not overburdened with children or pregnancy, putting both herself and her children at risk. It is noteworthy then that in many such harems wet-nurses were employed, thereby allowing the harem women to resume ovulation soon after the birth of a child.

This connection between status, wealth and sex is quite common in the historical record. From the tyrants of old to the presidents of democracies today, when men become rich and powerful enough they pursue and achieve polygyny either through taking many wives or concubines or, in cultures where polygyny is outlawed, extramarital affairs.

Exactly why extreme polygyny faded is unclear. Matt Ridley argues that the extreme polygyny of harems seems to represent an interlude between the end of hunter-gathering and the spread of democracy (Ridley, 1993). Harems among hunter-gatherers would have been difficult to sustain for the reasons given earlier. But come the Neolithic revolution, the accumulation of power and wealth in the hands of a few and the growth of a hierarchical ruling elite, then they become physically and politically feasible. The spread of democracy then undermines the privileges of the ruling class and extramarital intercourse is pursued by more subtle means.

The behaviour of autocrats such as those outlined above shows that individuals will exploit their positions to increase their reproductive success. Since men are biologically capable of fathering more offspring than any one woman could supply, it is no surprise that harems were designed for men. There are no known cases of female rulers setting up harems of young men or 'toy boys'. Sexual behaviour is therefore a product of culture and biology. Some cultures permitted the formation of harems and the sexual propensities of males gave them a biological rationale.

The female perspective

We must be cautious of examining mating solely from the male perspective. Females have their own reproductive interests at stake and are not simply passive receptacles for male success. If we remember that in polygyny some males will have many mates and some none, we could ask what makes a female agree to polygyny when she could presumably mate monogamously with one of the males left over. In making such a decision, the female has a set of costs and benefits to assess. The costs of mating with an already-mated male compared to an unmated male might include the obligation to share resources offered by the polygynous male with other females, and, more generally, coping with rivalry from other females. The benefits might be that the female collects a set of successful genes since the abilities of the men who are successful and wealthy enough (perhaps as a result of strength, intelligence or ability to command the loyalty of others) to take many wives are likely to have at least some genetic basis. The male offspring of a female who chooses such a man will inherit their father's genes. If they too become successful then the number of her grandchildren is increased. An additional benefit might be that the female acquires access to high-quality resources that likewise help the survival chances of her offspring, more than compensating for the fact that they are shared. A remark attributed to the former American politician Henry Kissinger is instructive here, when he said that 'power is the greatest aphrodisiac'.

Among non-human animals there are plenty of examples of females copulating with more than one male in a season or a lifetime. True polyandry, however, in the form of a lasting relationship between one female and several males where the sex roles are reversed and males assume parental responsibilities, is very rare. At first sight, polyandry would appear to be a bad deal for both males and females. From the female's perspective, sperm from one male is sufficient to fertilise all her eggs, so why bother to mate with more than one male? From the male perspective it is even worse: a male supplying parental care to rearing offspring that are not his own is, in a genetic sense, wasting his time.

As noted earlier, cultural surveys suggest that most human societies are mildly polygynous or monogamous, with very few polyandrous human societies. One of the best-documented examples of polyandry is the Tre-ba people of Tibet, where two brothers may share a wife. One reason for this unusual arrangement seems to be as a means of avoiding the split of a family landholding in a harsh environment where a family unit must be of a certain minimum size to thrive, and where the local tax system militates against the division of property. This is not simply a reversal of polygyny, however. Men are socially dominant over women and the younger brother's ambition is to obtain his own wife, and, as in most societies, Tre-ba men acquire wives, not the other way round (Crook and Crook, 1988). Moreover, when a Tre-ba family has daughters but not sons then polygyny is practised whereby the daughters share a husband and the family holding is passed on through them.

The fact that stable polyandry is rare does not mean that it does not take place in a more discreet fashion. One highly successful strategy from a female point of view is to mate with a man who is wealthy, successful and who cares for her children, while at the same time shopping around for good genes through extramarital affairs. This may sound very cynical but we should remember two things. First, the whole process is not really articulated at a conscious level. A women who is attracted to a dashing, physically attractive and intelligent man during extramarital affairs is not really thinking that his genes would be a useful set to pair with her own. Secondly, natural selection is not a moral process. It has provided us with ways to survive and reproduce, some of which we may later decide are ethically questionable.

So far we have examined the differences between male and female mating strategies based on an examination of contemporary tribal cultures, patterns observed in historical societies and expectations based on the biological differences between men and women. To develop a more detailed picture of human sexual behaviour we need to examine the force of sexual selection, and to this we turn in the next chapter.

Summary

- An evolutionary approach to human sexuality helps us to understand the mating strategies pursued by ancestral and contemporary males and females. Humans evolved to their present state largely in hunter-gathering groups. An inspection of such groups may help us to establish what species-typical mating behaviour is likely.
- At a superficial level, the mating behaviour of animals can be described in terms of species-characteristic mating systems such as monogamy, polygyny and polyandry. A deeper understanding is gained, however, by looking at the strategies pursued by individuals as they strive to maximise their reproductive success.

- Humans are like many mammals in the sense that females limit the reproductive success of males. The large harems created for the exclusive use of ancient despots and emperors show that under some conditions males can behave opportunistically to achieve an extreme degree of polygyny.

Review exercise

Fill in the blanks in the following sentences using the terms listed at the end.

In the breeding season northern elephant seals form groups such that one male has exclusive sexual access to several females. The females only mate with this bull male. We can say that the male is _____ while the females are _____.

In Western society the marriage contract is an expression of a _____ bond. However, adultery is common and often a reason for divorce. A male committing adultery could be said to be behaving _____. A female committing adultery is displaying _____.

From a biological point of view, a harem can be viewed as a mechanism for a ruler to ____ the spread of his _____.

Terms (one term is used twice)

maximise, monogamous, polygynously, polyandry, polygynous, genes

Further reading

Betzig, L. (ed.) (1997). *Human Nature: A Critical Reader*. Oxford: Oxford University Press. A useful book that contains numerous original articles on human sexuality together with a critique in retrospect by the original authors.

Cartwright, J. (2000). *Evolution and Human Behaviour*. London: Macmillan. Although designed for undergraduates, Chapter 4 of this book is especially relevant to the chapter here and should be of use to the good A-level candidate.

Potts, M. and Short, R. (1999). *Ever Since Adam and Eve: The evolution of human sexuality*. Cambridge, UK: Cambridge University Press. A beautifully illustrated book. Humane in its approach.

3

Sexual selection

Natural selection and sexual selection compared
Inter- and intrasexual selection
Parental investment
Potential reproductive rates: humans and other animals
The operational sex ratio
Consequences of sexual selection
Summary

Natural selection and sexual selection compared

Darwin's idea of natural selection was that animals should end up with physical and behavioural characteristics that allow them to perform well in the ordinary processes of life such as competing with their rivals, finding food, avoiding predators and finding a mate. Most features of plants and animals should, therefore, have some adaptive function in the struggle for existence. As noted earlier in relation to Figure 1.1, the life and death of thousands of our ancestors should have ensured that by now our characteristics are finely tuned to growth, survival and reproduction. Nature should allow no extravagance or waste. So what about, for example, the spectacular train of the peacock? It does not help a peacock fly any faster or better. Neither is it used to fight rivals or deter predators – in fact, the main predator of peafowl, the tiger, seems particularly adept at pulling down peacocks by their tails. It would seem to be an irrelevance, a magnificent one to be sure, but nevertheless an encumbrance that should have been eliminated by natural selection long before now. Nor is the peacock's tail an exception: many species of animals are characterised by one sex (usually the male) possessing some colourful adornment that serves no apparent function (or even seems dysfunctional), while the other sex, like the peahen, seems much more sensibly designed. Such features seem, at first glance, to challenge the power of natural selection to explain the behaviour of animals.

When males and females differ like this in some physical characteristic, they are said to be **sexually dimorphic** (lit.: two shapes). Sexual dimorphism is found to varying degrees in the animal kingdom. Humans are moderately dimorphic: men are, on average, taller than women and more muscular, and grow more facial hair. Now some of these differences could in principle be due to natural selection: males and females may exploit different food resources and female mammals are generally adapted to provide more care to offspring than males. If ancestral men hunted while women stayed at home nurturing children (albeit a rather oversimplified picture) then height and muscularity would have benefited males more than females. Yet, however ingeniously we work to apply the principle of natural selection, we are still drawn back by the startling spectacle of the peacock's tail.

It was Darwin himself who provided the answer to this seeming paradox. In his *Descent of Man and Selection in Relation to Sex* (1871), he gave the explanation that is still accepted (with refinements) today. Darwin realised that the force of natural selection must be complemented by the force of sexual selection: individuals possess features that make them attractive to members of the opposite sex or help them compete with members of the same sex for access to mates. In essence, the train of the peacock has been shaped for the delectation of the peahen. For reasons that are still obscure, peahens are excited by males with fancy tails. Natural and sexual selection now form the twin pillars of the Darwinian programme that seeks to demonstrate how the features of organisms have evolved (sometimes called the 'adaptationist paradigm').

Darwin used the illustration shown in Figure 3.1 in his second edition of *The Descent of Man and Selection in Relation to Sex* (1874). The male is the one with the long and highly ornamented tail. Darwin realised that the tail grew like this to please the female and so help the male gain a sexual partner.

Figure 3.1 Sexual selection as found in the hummingbird species *Sparthura underwoodi*. Darwin used this illustration in his second edition of *The Descent of Man and Selection in Relation to Sex* (1874). The male is the one with the long and highly ornamented tail. Darwin realised that the tail grew like this to please the female and so help the male gain a sexual partner

Inter- and intrasexual selection

We should really distinguish between two types of sexual selection: 'intra' and 'inter'. Even among species where polygamy is the norm, the sex ratio (males: females) usually remains close to 1:1; in other words, the number of males and females in a population is roughly the same. So where conditions favour polygyny males must compete with other males for access to females; this follows from the obvious reason that if each male is intent on mating with two or more females to the exclusion of other males then there simply are not enough females to go round. This leads to **intrasexual selection** (intra = within). Intrasexual competition can take place prior to mating or, in the case of **sperm competition** (see below), after copulation has taken place. On the other hand, for many species a female investing heavily in offspring, or only capable of raising a few offspring in a season or lifetime, needs to make sure she has made the right choice. There will probably be no shortage of males clamouring for her attention but the implications of a wrong choice for the female are graver than for the male, who may, after all, be seeking other partners anyway. A female under these conditions can afford to be choosy and pick what she thinks is the best male. This leads to **intersexual selection** (inter = between).

This distinction between intra- and intersexual selection helps us to begin to understand some of the more bizarre manifestations of sexual activity in the natural world. The headbutting and twisting of antlers of male deer in the rutting season, while the females look on, is an example of intrasexual selection: males compete with males for the prize of impregnating many females. The screeching displays of the peacock in front of a demure and far less brightly coloured peahen is an example of intersexual selection: the female chooses the male with the most elaborate and impressive train (tail). We now need to consider how these concepts help us understand human sexual behaviour.

Parental investment

As a very rough guide, the degree of discrimination exercised by an individual in selecting a partner is related to the degree of commitment and investment that is made by both parties. Male black grouse that provide no paternal care will mate with anything that resembles a female black grouse. Female black grouse, however, which bear the brunt of the consequences of fertilisation in terms of egg production and incubation, are rather more careful in their choices, and select what they take to be the most suitable male from those displaying before them. Among humans, both males and females have a highly developed sense of physical beauty and this aesthetic sensibility is consistent with a high degree of both maternal and paternal investment. The more investment an individual makes, the more important it becomes to choose its mate carefully – genes that direct for poor choices (e.g. infertile or unhealthy individuals) are destined to be eliminated from the gene pool. All this decision-making results in the selective force of intersexual selection. It follows that if a high degree of investment by one sex sets up the force of intersexual selection, then the lack of investment by the other sets up competition between that sex for access to the sex that invests most. These ideas were formalised into the concept of **parental investment** by Robert Trivers in 1972.

The concept of parental investment seemed to promise, and indeed to a degree did deliver, a coherent and plausible way of examining the relationship between parental investment, sexual selection and mating behaviour. The sex that invests least will compete over the sex that invests most, and the sex that invests most will have more to lose by a poor match and so will be choosier over its choice of partner. Trivers defined parental investment as

> any investment by the parent in an individual offspring that increases the offspring's chance of surviving (and hence reproductive success) at the cost of the parent's ability to invest in other offspring. (Trivers, 1972)

Using this definition, Trivers concluded that the **optimum** or ideal number of offspring for each parent would be different. In the case of many mammals, a low-investing male will have the potential to sire more offspring than a single female could produce. A male could, therefore, increase his reproductive success by increasing the number of his copulations. On the other hand, females should prefer quality rather than quantity.

The logic is clear but in practice it has proved difficult to measure such terms as increase in 'offspring's chance of surviving' and 'costs to parents'. Consequently, deciding which sex invests the most is not always easy. One concept that may help to circumvent these difficulties is that of potential reproductive rates.

Potential reproductive rates: humans and other animals

Clutton-Brock and Vincent (1991) have suggested that a fruitful way of understanding the mating behaviour of animals is to focus on the potential offspring production rate of males and females, rather than trying to measure mating effort or parental investment. In this view it becomes important to identify the sex which is acting as a 'reproductive bottleneck' for the other. Applying these ideas to human mating, it should be clear by now that there are large differences between the potential reproductive rates of men and women. Harems may have been common in ancient civilizations but there are no examples recorded of female rulers guarding a company of male studs or 'toy boys'. Biologically, what would be the point?

It is noteworthy then that the record often claimed for the largest number of children from one parent is 888 for a man and 69 for a woman. The father was Ismail the Bloodthirsty (1672–1727), an Emperor of Morocco. The mother was a Russian lady who experienced 27 pregnancies with a high number of twins and triplets. Most people are more astonished by the female record than the male.

The figure of 888 looks extreme compared to most cases of fatherhood but would at first glance seem to be a practical possibility. Ismail died at the age of about 82 and could have enjoyed a period of fertility of at least 55 years. Over this time, he could have had sex with his concubines once or twice daily. The performance claimed for Ismail has recently been questioned, however, by Dorothy Einon of University College London (Einon, 1998). Einon analysed the mathematical probability of conception by members of his harem and concluded that 888 children may be an exaggerated figure. The problem for a man with access to a large number of females and intent on breeding is that he is uncertain when his womenfolk are ovulating. The fact that ovulation takes place between 14 and 18 days before the next menstruation was not known until 1920. Before this, men knew that sex led to offspring but not when sex was at its most effective. Einon has argued that the viability of sperm inside the female genital tract is only 3.5 days, giving a potentially fertile period of 3.5 days within each month. More recently, the reputation of Moulay Ismail has been restored somewhat by Gould (2000), who points to errors in Einon's analysis – he lived until about 82 for example, not 55 as Einon thought, and sperm remains viable for 6 days, not 3.5. Gould concludes that Moulay Ismail could have fathered 888 children if he sustained a rate of 1.2 couplings per day over 62 years – an exhausting prospect but not beyond the bounds of possibility.

It is possible of course that men know subconsciously when ovulation is taking place and are thereby able to better target their reproductive efforts. Males may produce 280 million sperm with each ejaculate (enough to fertilise the entire female population of the USA if all were viable), but most are wasted in that they fail to meet an egg.

The obvious question is why women have evolved to conceal ovulation. If they behaved like chimps then a red swelling and obvious odours would announce the fact unambiguously and the social life of humans would be vastly different. This feature of human sexuality illustrates once again that behaviour is not designed to benefit the species but to serve the individual. Although concealed ovulation is still a puzzle in evolutionary biology, it now seems likely that it may have evolved as a tactic by females to elicit more care and attention from males than they would otherwise give.

We should also note that most men in history have not been emperors, and the harems enjoyed by Ismail and his like would not have been a regular feature of our evolutionary past. It is probably true to say, however, that in *Homo sapiens* the limiting factor in reproduction resides marginally with the female. This by itself would predict some male–male competition and both intra- and intersexual selection can be expected to have moulded the human psyche.

The operational sex ratio

The potential reproductive rate and the operational sex ratio are closely related concepts. Although for most mammals there are roughly equal numbers of males and females, not all of the males or females may be sexually active and there may be local variations in the ratio of the sexes. This idea is contained in the concept of the operational sex ratio:

$$\text{Operational sex ratio} = \frac{\text{Fertilisable females}}{\text{Sexually active males}}$$

When this ratio is high, the reproductive bottleneck rests with males and females could compete with other females for the available males. When the ratio is low, the situation is reversed and males will vie with other males for the sexual favours of fewer females (Figure 3.2).

At first sight, it would seem that females are always the limiting resource for male fecundity. Consider the following facts. If you are a young fertile male, while you are reading this you are producing sperm at the phenomenal rate of about 3000 per second. If you are a young fertile female you are holding on to a lifetime's supply of only 400 eggs. In addition, a man could impregnate a different woman every day for a year whereas over this same period a woman can become pregnant

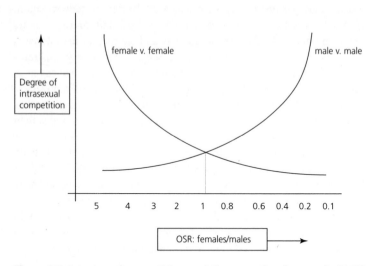

Figure 3.2 **Intrasexual competition and the operational sex ratio (OSR) (adapted from Kvarnemo and Ahnesjo, 1996)**

only once. We need to consider this with caution, however. Imagine a male that mates with 56 different women over 56 days and a female that mates with 56 different men over the same period. The woman is likely to become pregnant and bear one offspring in the same year. Using the reasoning advanced by Einon earlier, if the male avoids the time of menstruation he has about a 15% chance of impregnating a woman during her fertile period. Only half of the female ovarian cycles will be fertile, some women will be infertile themselves anyway, and implantation will only take place about 40% of the time. The number of women a man could expect to make pregnant is one. Over a year this could be raised to about six (365/56 = 6.5). Women are in one sense a limiting resource but not to the extremes that might be indicated by the differences in the size or rate of production of gametes.

The operational sex ratio (females/males) for a group of humans with a 1:1 sex ratio (i.e. equal numbers of men and women in the population) will be less than one if we measure it in terms of males or females that are fertile. It is likely that there will be more sexually fertile males than females. This arises from the fact that men experience a longer period of fertility compared to women. It is counterbalanced somewhat by the higher mortality rates for men than women, but not entirely. The picture is complicated, however, if the population is growing. Under these circumstances the fact that women tend to prefer to marry slightly older men will mean more younger women than there are slightly older men available, since the cohort of marriageable men will be smaller than the number of marriageable women in the expanding cohort below. Guttentag and Secord (1983) have argued that this in itself can be a contributing factor to the development of social mores. In the USA from 1965 to the 1970s, because of the postwar baby boom, there was an oversupply of women compared to the cohort of slightly older men. This would have the effect of decreasing male–male competition and increasing female–female competition. This allowed men to pursue their own reproductive preferences, especially in terms of an increased number of partners, to a greater extent than women could pursue theirs. These authors suggest that this could be a contributing factor to the liberal sexual mores of those decades characterised by high divorce rates, lower levels of paternal investment and a relaxed attitude to sex. They stress that sex ratios by themselves are not a sufficient cause for such social changes but may be part of the equation (Guttentag and Secord, 1983).

Such arguments are extremely difficult to support conclusively. Following the Second World War other more profound changes occurred in Western cultures, such as rising affluence and, crucially, the availability of the contraceptive pill. An interesting study could be made on the changes in social values in France, Britain and Germany following the First World War, when the carnage of war would have biased the sex ratio towards females. Here again, however, other changes were taking place, such as votes for women, changes in the economic status of women and so forth. Perhaps a more realistic application of sex ratio thinking may be found in the analysis of traditional cultures where social values shift less rapidly. In South America, there are two indigenous Indian groups with different sex ratios. The Hiwi tribe shows a surplus of men, while the Ache people have a sex ratio of females:males of about 1.5 (Hill and Hurtado, 1996). The ecology of the two groups is otherwise similar, but whereas among the Ache people extramarital affairs are common and marriages are unstable, among the Hiwi marital life is more stable. This pattern is what one would expect from the anticipated effect of sex ratios on mating strategies.

In virtually all cultures, however, it is significant that men engage in competitive display tactics and are more likely to take risks than women are. It is also men who tend to pay for sex, this being one way of increasing the supply of the limiting resource (Figure 3.3).

Figure 3.3 Detail from *The Rake's Progress* by William Hogarth. Here the young rake (a man of loose morals) is shown visiting a brothel. Prostitution is said to be the world's oldest profession. The fact that the vast majority of prostitution consists of women exchanging sex for money from men is understandable from an evolutionary standpoint, since women are the limiting resource for men. Consequently, men will seek ways to improve the supply of the limiting resource

Consequences of sexual selection

Just as natural selection has left humans with bodies and brains suited to the processes of finding food, avoiding predators and resisting disease, so sexual selection has left its mark on our bodies and our sexual inclinations. So much so, that once we understand the basic ideas of sexual selection we can examine humans and make predictions about what type of sexual behaviour patterns may be typical of our species.

Sexual dimorphism in body size

Darwin argued that intrasexual selection was bound to favour the evolution of a variety of special adaptations, such as weapons, defensive organs, sexual differences in size and shape and a whole range of devices to threaten or deter rivals (Figure 3.4). The importance of size is illustrated by a number of seal species. During the breeding season male northern elephant seals (*Mirounga angustirostris*) rush towards each other and engage in a contest of head-butting. Such fighting has led to a strong selection pressure in favour of size, and consequently male seals are several times larger than females. Elephant seals are in fact among the most sexually dimorphic of all animals. Among *M. angustirostris* a typical male is about three times heavier than a typical female. The mating system of these seals is described as female defence polygyny and a male needs to be large both to fight off contenders to take his place among a harem of females and to defend his position once he is there. As a result of the intense competition, many males die before reaching adulthood without ever having mated.

Humans show sexual dimorphism in a range of traits. Men, for example have greater upper body strength and more facial and body hair than do women. Men also have deeper voices, later sexual maturity and experience a higher risk of infant mortality than do females. The pattern of fat distribution between men and women is also different. Women tend to deposit fat more on the buttocks and hips than do men. These of course refer to average tendencies. It is likely that many of these are the results of sexual selection.

The fact that human infants need prolonged care would ensure that females were alert to the abilities of males to provide resources. In addition, the fact that a female invests considerably in each offspring would make mistakes (in the form of weak or sickly offspring that are unlikely to reproduce) very expensive. It has been estimated that human females of the Old Stone Age would have only raised successfully to adulthood two or three children. Females would therefore be on the lookout for males who show signs of being genetically fit and healthy and who are able to provide resources. Both these attributes, genetic and material, would ensure that her offspring receive a good start in life.

One possible way in which men and women could assess the genetic fitness of a potential mate is through the symmetry of their features.

Figure 3.4 Sexual dimorphism in the beetle species *Chasognathus grantii*. The male has long protruding mandibles, which it uses to fight and intimidate other males. The female, illustrated in the lower half of the diagram, lacks these characters. Darwin concluded that although these devices were selected for fighting they seemed to be excessive in size even for this purpose and noted that 'the suspicion has crossed my mind that they may in addition serve as an ornament'. Diagram from *The Descent of Man and Selection in Relation to Sex* (1874)

The logic here is that symmetry is an honest signal since it is difficult to fake and physiologically difficult to achieve. Invasion by parasites and vulnerability to environmental stress factors both reduce the symmetry of an organism. Only the fittest genomes are capable of engineering symmetry in the body of an animal. Evidence that humans are sensitive to symmetry in their appraisal of the attractiveness of mates comes from work on facial attractiveness explored in Chapter 4.

Sexual enthusiasm

Another physiological characteristic that can assist males is 'sexual enthusiasm' or the capacity to be easily sexually stimulated. As expected, the males of many polygynous species have a low threshold for sexual arousal. Some species of frog in the mating season will cling to anything that resembles a female frog, and males will often attempt to mate with the wrong species and even the wrong sex. Another feature of the sex drive of the male is the 'Coolidge effect', so named after US President Coolidge. The story goes that while visiting a farm President and Mrs Coolidge were shown a yard containing many hens and only one cockerel. When Mrs Coolidge asked why only one cockerel was necessary she was told that he could copulate many times each day. 'Please tell that to the President', she said. When the President was informed he asked if the cockerel copulated with the same hen and was told no. His reply was 'Tell that to Mrs Coolidge' (Goodenough et al., 1993). The Coolidge effect has been observed in many species. In a study on Norway rats (*Rattus norvegicus*), Fisher (1962) found that whereas a male rat with a single female reached sexual satiation after about 1.5 hours, some males could be kept sexually active for up to 8 hours by the introduction of novel females at appropriate intervals.

Adult magazines

An inspection of the top shelf of many newsagents often reveals a selection of adult magazines. The vast majority of these are purchased by men and contain pictures of women in various stages of undress. There are few adult magazines that are targeted at women.

Some people explain this by reference to social and cultural factors while others invoke explanations from evolutionary psychology. Suggest an explanation for this phenomenon that falls into each of these categories. Try to think of a way you could further test each explanation.

Progress exercise

Post-copulatory intrasexual competition: sperm competition

At first glance it may seem that once copulation has taken place then intrasexual competition must cease: one male must surely have won. But the natural world has more surprises in store. Some females mate with many males and retain sperm in their reproductive tracts; sperm from two or more males may then compete inside the female to fertilise her egg. The concept of sperm competition illuminates many features of male and female anatomy in non-human animals. Male insects have evolved a variety of devices aimed at neutralising or displacing sperm already present in the female. The male damselfly (*Calopteryx maculata*), for example, has evolved a penis designed to both transfer sperm and, by means of backward-pointing hairs on the horn of the penis, remove any sperm already in the female from a rival male.

Many animals have also evolved other tactics to outwit rivals in sperm competition. When a male garter snake mates with a female it leaves behind a thick guey mass, technically known as a copulatory plug, that effectively seals off the reproductive tract of the female from other would-be suitors. When a male wolf mates with a female its penis becomes so enlarged that even after ejaculation it remains stuck in the vagina of the female for up to half an hour after impregnation. The male and female remain fixed like this in some apparent discomfort, but the mechanism ensures that the sperm of the successful male gets a head start over any rivals.

We should not think of females as passive in this process of sperm competition. The female may exercise choice over the sperm once it is inside her (Wirtz, 1997). Many female insects store sperm that they use to fertilise their eggs at oviposition (egg-laying) as the eggs pass down the female's reproductive tract. It has been suggested that the function of the female orgasm in humans is to assist the take-up of sperm towards the cervix (Baker and Bellis, 1995). Randy Thornhill and his workers carried out a study to show that the bodily symmetry of the male is a strong predictor of whether or not a female will experience a copulatory orgasm. Symmetry is thought to be an indicator of genetic fitness and the possession of a good **immune system** (Thornhill *et al*., 1994). The orgasm therefore ensures that sperm from exciting and desirable males, who presumably are genetically fit and unlikely to be transmitting a disease, stand a good chance of meeting with the female's egg. In this way the human female may be extending her choice beyond courtship (Baker and Bellis, 1995).

The more sperm produced the greater is the chance of at least one finding the egg of the female: 50 million sperm are twice as effective as 25 million and so on. In species where sperm competition is rife, we would expect males to increase the number of sperm produced or ejaculated compared to species where sperm competition is less intense. Between species, this prediction has been supported indirectly by measurements on levels of sperm expenditure as measured by testis size. Species facing intense sperm competition have larger testes than those where sperm competition is less pronounced (see section on 'Testis size' in Chapter 4).

Baker and Bellis at Manchester University provide evidence to support the idea that the number of sperm in the ejaculate of men is adjusted according to the probability of sperm competition taking place. In one study, when couples spent all their time together over a given period the male was found to ejaculate about 389×10^6 sperm during a subsequent sexual act. When the couples only spent 5% of their time together men typically ejaculated 712×10^6 sperm. Baker and Bellis interpret this as consistent with the idea that the male increases the number of sperm in the latter case to compete more effectively against rival sperm which may have entered the female if she had been unfaithful. Baker and Bellis have been successful in generating new ideas in an area of research that faces innumerable experimental and ethical difficulties (Baker and Bellis, 1995). They have also been successful in disseminating their ideas, helped partly by a media eager for such theories and partly by the popularisation of their work in such books as *Sperm Wars* (Baker, 1996).

In the 'sperm wars' of post-ejaculate intrasexual competition, males can adopt various tactics: they can produce sperm in large numbers, attempt to displace rival sperm, insert copulatory plugs or produce sperm that actively seek out to destroy rivals. Baker and Bellis (1995) have developed this latter idea into a 'kamikaze sperm hypothesis', claiming that a wide variety of animals including humans produce sperm whose function is to block or destroy rival sperm. Part of the evidence used by Baker and Bellis is the number of deformed sperm found in any ejaculate. They argue that the function of some of these deformed sperm is to seek out and destroy sperm from rival males.

Following the initial publication of the ideas of Baker and Bellis in 1988 considerable debate ensued concerning the existence of these kamikaze sperm. In one study, sperm from different males was mixed *in vitro* (i.e. in glassware in laboratory conditions) and its viability compared to sperm mixed from the same male. If the kamikaze sperm hypothesis is correct then mixed male sperm should show signs of lack of function as rival sperm kill each other off. The result, however, was that the performance of mixed male sperm was not noticeably different from that of same-male sperm (Moore, Martin and Birkhead, 1999). In a careful analysis of the evidence, Harcourt (1991) concluded that kamikaze sperm did not in all probability exist, and that 'the function of all mammalian sperm is to fertilise, and that sperm competition in mammals occurs through scramble competition, not contest competition' (Harcourt, 1991, p. 314). Harcourt's conclusion is based on the fact, among others, that male primates in polyandrous species (i.e. where a female will mate with more than one male) do not produce more deformed (i.e. non-fertilising) sperm than primates in monandrous (one male, one female) species. Yet if the kamikaze hypothesis were to be correct this is the reversal of what would be expected. Harcourt does agree, however, that the males of many mammalian species produce secretions from accessory glands that serve to coagulate semen and act as a copulatory plug.

Long before sperm competition takes place, however, a male has to be accepted by a female or vice versa. Passing this quality control procedure has also left its mark on the anatomy and behaviour of humans and to this process we now turn.

Good genes and honest signals

Darwin had difficulty in explaining in adaptationist terms why females find certain features attractive. A peahen may have forced male peafowl to sport long trains to please her but why, in functional or ultimate terms, should she be pleased by a long rather than a short tail? If, as Darwinism informs us, beauty is in the eye of the genes, what genetic self-interest is served by finding long trains or colourful tails beautiful? If we can crack this problem then perhaps the basis of human physical beauty can be understood. Answers to this puzzle tend to fall into two camps: the 'good-sense' and the 'good-taste' schools of thought (Cronin, 1991).

The good-taste school of thought stems from the ideas of Fisher, who investigated the problem in the 1930s. Consider a male character such as tail length that females once found attractive for sound evolutionary reasons, such as it indicated the species and sex of the male, or it showed the male was healthy enough to grow a good-sized tail. Fisher argued that under some conditions a runaway effect could result, leading to longer and longer tails. Such conditions could be that some time in the past an arbitrary (i.e. non-functional) drift of preference led a large number of females in a population to prefer long tails. Once this fashion took hold it could become self-reinforcing. Any female that resisted the trend, and mated with a male with a shorter tail, would leave sons with short tails that were unattractive. Females that succumbed to the fashion would leave 'sexy sons' with long tails and daughters with the same preference for long tails. The overall effect is to saddle males with increasingly longer tails, until the sheer expense of producing them outweighs any benefit in attracting females. The argument and the precise conditions under which this mechanism could work are complex, but evolutionary biologists are now convinced that the Fisherian runaway process is a distinct possibility. In this model, although individuals are choosing a set of genes by examining a feature such as a long tail that is expressed by such genes, the genes are not necessarily good for anything else. In a sense they have become an arbitrary fashion accessory to which individuals find themselves attracted.

The 'good-sense' view suggests that an animal estimates the quality of the genotype of a prospective mate through the signals he or she sends out prior to mating. In addition, individuals could also assess each other on the basis of the level of resources a mate is likely to be able to provide – something that in itself could be a reflection of the quality of genes that an animal carries. These ideas are now some of the most promising lines of inquiry in sexual selection theory with many suggestive applications to human mate choice (Table 3.1).

The '**good genes**' dimension of good sense would explain why in polygynous mating systems females share a mate with many other females, even though there may be plenty of males without partners, and despite the fact that the males of many species contribute nothing in the way of resources or parental care. Females are in effect look-ing for good genes. The fact that the male is donating them to any willing female is of no concern to her. The important point here is that the female is able to judge the quality of the male's genotype from the 'honest signals' he is forced to send. In this respect, size, bodily condition, symmetry and social status are all signals provid-ing the female with information about the potential of her mate.

Table 3.1 Mechanisms of intersexual competition	
Category	**Mechanism**
Good taste (Fisherian runaway process)	Initial female preference becomes self-reinforcing. A runaway effect results that leads to elaborate and often dysfunctional (in terms of natural selection) traits, e.g. peacock's train
Good sense (genes and/or resources)	One sex uses signals from the other to estimate the quality of the genome on offer. Such signals may indicate desirable characteristics such as resistance to parasites or general metabolic efficiency. One partner may also inspect resources held by the other and the likelihood that such resources will be made available

Likewise, some human females find some men sexually attractive, even though they know such men may be unreliable, philandering and untrustworthy.

There are several ways in which features of an animal may serve as signals of genetic prowess. Males and females can send signals about their health and reproductive status in a variety of ways. Consider the time-honoured principle of fashion that 'if you have it flaunt it; if you haven't, hide it'. This applies to cosmetics as much as clothes. This leads to a distinction between honest and dishonest signals. Hiding signs of genetic weakness or false advertising are really **dishonest signals**. Dishonest signals are rare among non-human animals since they are likely to be spotted and eliminated in favour of honest ones. Humans, however, with their clever brains and sophisticated culture, are particularly adept at sending both honest and dishonest signals about themselves to others.

A particularly fruitful line of research that has emerged in recent years is costly signalling theory (CST). This theory suggests that honest signals will emerge and be attended to by the receiver if one or both of the following conditions hold:

- The signal must be honestly linked to the quality of the trait it is trying to advertise. When this is the case imitation by inferior individuals is impossible since the linkage would ensure that the advertisement actually revealed the poor quality of the signaller.
- The signal must be a handicap, i.e. it must impose a cost on the signaller. In this way only high-quality individuals can afford the handicap and hence advertise.

Smith and Bird are anthropologists in the USA who have applied this theory with some success to turtle hunting among the Meriam islanders of Torres Strait, Australia. The Meriam people live on the barrier reef island of Mer, about 100 miles from New Guinea. They have numerous public feasts during which time men engage in competitive dancing, hunting, diving and boat racing. During one type of feast involving funerary rites, large amounts of turtle meat are consumed. To provide this meat turtles have to be hunted, and turtle hunting seems to qualify as an example of a costly and honest signal since:

1. Hunting involves taking a small boat out to sea, locating a turtle and then jumping on its back with a harpoon – a procedure that requires strength and agility and is physically dangerous.
2. When the turtles are captured, they are shared communally during a public feast. In fact the hunters take virtually no share of the meat and have to bear the full cost of the hunt themselves.
3. During the feast, people are attentive to who provided the largest turtles and who returned with small ones or none at all.

In short, the ability to return with a large turtle and offer it as a communal gift is an honest advertisement of physical strength and vigour as well as wealth. It is difficult to see how a physically unfit and resource-poor male could return from the hunt with a large turtle. The fact that the hunt is a signal rather than an economic necessity is indicated by the fact that this sort of hunting is too risky to be pursued except during public feasting. In other words, the activity does not make much economic sense except as a device for young men to show off their virtues (Smith and Bliege Bird, 2000).

Using the table below speculate on the signals that humans send each other. Try to add more honest and dishonest signals to the table and suggest the function that they serve. As a hint, fashion in clothes, cosmetics, high-risk sports and competitions, and displays of wealth are likely candidates for this sort of treatment.

Honest signal	Functional (adaptive) significance
Clothes to emphasise narrow waist	Indicates youth, fertility and the fact that the woman is not pregnant
Dishonest signal	Deception suggested
Shoulder pads in a man's suit	Suggests upper body strength and musculature – potentially attractive features to women

In some species, the males provide nothing except a few drops of sperm. The females have come to expect nothing except genes, so if they are choosy it will be for good genes rather than any parental after-sales service. Most human females, however, expect males to bring something to mating in addition to their DNA, and may judge, therefore, the ability of the male to provide resources before and after copulation. In the case of humans, resources could be indicated by the social and financial status of a male and, just as importantly, his willingness to donate them in a caring relationship. This could of course be one of the functions of courtship in human societies. As well as allowing an assessment of character and health, courtship, viewed in this dispassionate light, also enables each sex to 'weigh up' their prospective partner in terms of their commitment to a relationship and the resources they are likely to bring, both genetic and material.

There is little doubt that wealth is sexy. In modern societies the phenomenon of the 'sugar daddy' is well known. Rich and powerful men seem to be able to attract younger and highly attractive females as their partners. One British chat show host caused great mirth when she asked the younger attractive wife of a wealthy and well-known TV star, 'Tell me Mrs ___ , what first attracted you to your millionaire husband?' This dimension to human mating will be visited again in the study of advertisements for partners (see section on 'Surveys using published advertisements' in Chapter 4).

Summary

- Sexual selection results when individuals compete for mates. Competition within one sex for access to the other is termed intrasexual selection. Intersexual selection gives rise to selection pressures that favour large size and differences in size between the sexes (sexual dimorphism).
- Individuals of one sex also compete with each other to satisfy the requirements laid down by the other sex. An individual may require, for example, some demonstration or signal of genetic fitness or the possession or command of resources. Selective pressures resulting from the choosiness of one sex for the other are studied under the heading of intersexual selection.
- The precise form that mating competition takes (such as which sex competes for the other) is related to the relative investments made by each sex and the ratio of fertile males to females. If females, by virtue of their heavy investments in offspring for example, act as reproductive bottlenecks for males, then males will compete with males for access to females. In these conditions females can be expected to be discriminating in their choice of mates.
- Sperm competition is a special case of intrasexual selection. The large number of sperm produced by human males and the evidence that some types of sperm seem to attack foreign sperm are consistent with a view that sperm competition has been a factor in our evolution.

- Men and women will both be on the lookout for honest signals of genetic worth from prospective partners. Features that males and females find attractive in members of the opposite sex should fall into the category of honest signals.

Review exercise

You have been given the task of writing the script for a David Attenborough style documentary on human sexual selection. You have chosen to use footage from cameras recording the way humans of both sexes intermingle and socialise in a student bar or coffee room. Write a short script of about 500 words in this style, making clear how the behaviour you observe (which within plausible limits you can make up based on your own experience) can be interpreted in terms of sexual selection theory.

Further reading

Barber, N. (1995). The evolutionary psychology of physical attractiveness: sexual selection and human morphology. *Ethology and Sociobiology* 16: 395–424. An excellent review of the literature on the significance of body shapes in men and women in relation to sexual selection.

Gould, J.L. and Gould, C.G. (1989). *Sexual Selection*. New York: Scientific American. Well illustrated and readable. Mostly about non-human animals but a short section at the end covers humans.

Hrdy, S.B. (1999). *Mother Nature*. London: Chatto & Windus. A wonderful book that considers the implications of evolution from a female perspective.

Ridley, M. (1993). *The Red Queen*. London: Viking. A delightful book that explores the nature of sexual selection and its application to humans.

Short, R. and Potts, M. (1999). *Ever Since Adam and Eve: The Evolution of Human Sexuality*. Cambridge, UK: Cambridge University Press. Superbly illustrated and authoritative work. A humane account of the evolution and significance of human sexuality.

Unravelling human sexuality

Comparisons between humans and other primates
Evolution of sexual desire: some expectations and approaches
Facial attractiveness
Sexual jealousy
Summary

Comparisons between humans and other primates

Mating behaviour has left its mark on the physical characteristics of primates such as humans and we are now in a position to apply some of the theory covered in earlier chapters to infer from the physical characteristics of modern humans the mating behaviour that shaped them. Two features of humans in particular are amenable to this type of analysis: the dimorphism in body size between men and women, and the size of men's testes.

Differences in body size between males and females

Figure 4.1 shows how body size dimorphism varies in relation to breeding systems for primates. The large difference between measures of dimorphism in monogamous and polygynous (single male) breeding systems can be explained by the more intense competition between males for females in the latter. The fact that dimorphism is seen in multi-male, multi-female groups (groups such as chimps containing many males and females) can probably be explained by the fact that

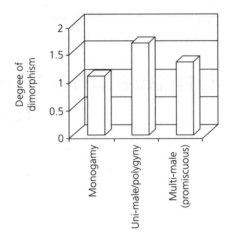

Figure 4.1 **Body size dimorphism (adult body weight of male divided by adult body weight of female) against mating system. Redrawn with permission from Clutton-Brock, T.H. and Harvey, P.H. (1984). Comparative approaches to investigating adaptation. In J.R. Krebs and N.B. Davies (eds) *Behavioural Ecology: An Evolutionary Approach*, 2nd edn (pp. 7–29). Blackwell Scientific Publications, Oxford**

in such groups competition takes place among males to secure their place in dominance hierarchies.

Testis size

The significance of testis size is that it indicates the degree of sperm competition (see section on 'sexual enthusiasm' in Chapter 3) in the species. It is expected that males will evolve large testes if they anticipate that their sperm will have to compete with other sperm in the female. Within these conditions the more sperm from a given male, the higher the chance it will become the father of the offspring. In the 1970s the biologist R.V. Short suggested that the differences in testis size for primates could be understood in terms of the intensity of sperm competition. To obtain reliable indicators, testis size has to be controlled for body weight since larger mammals will generally have larger testes to produce enough testosterone for the larger volume of blood in the animal, and a larger volume of ejaculate to counter the dilution effect of the larger reproductive tract of the female.

When these effects are controlled for, and relative testis size measured, the results support the suggestion of Short that relatively larger testes are selected for in multi-male groups where sperm competition will take place in the reproductive tract of the female. A single male in a harem does not need to produce as much sperm as a male in a multi-male group because in these conditions the male has exclusive access to the females in his harem. In such cases the contest for mates has taken place before mating and, consequently, rival sperm are unlikely to be a threat. In contrast, in promiscuous multi-male groups (chimps for example, Figure 4.2), females will mate with several males each day when in **oestrus** and successful males are those that, among other things, produce a lot of sperm (Figure 4.3).

Figure 4.2 **An adult male chimpanzee (*Pan troglodytes*). Zoologists agree that in evolutionary terms the common chimp is our nearest relative. We last shared a common ancestor with chimps about 7 million years ago. Photograph courtesy of Dr Lindsay Murray**

Testis size and bodily dimorphism applied to humans

Jared Diamond (1991) has called the theory of testis size and sperm competition 'one of the triumphs of modern physical anthropology' (p. 62). We are now in a position to apply it to humans.

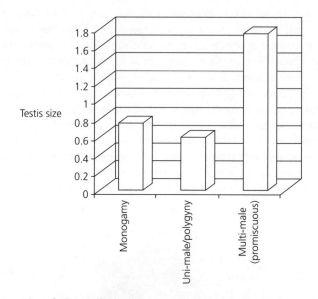

Figure 4.3 **Relative testis size against mating system. Error bars represent one standard error**

Note that the *y*-axis refers to deviations from the size of testes expected from a given primate body mass. Thus a value of 1 would indicate a testis size expected for an average primate of average body weight. Values above 1 indicate that testes are larger than would be expected. The values are for groups of animals in a genus rather than individual species. The difference between monogamous (P) and single male (S) groups is not significant, but both differ significantly from multi-male (M) (see Harcourt *et al.*, 1981)

Table 4.1 shows some key data on testis size and bodily dimorphism for the hominids (humans and the great apes) and orang-utans. We should first note that men are slightly heavier than women. This could reflect a number of features of our evolutionary ancestry. It could indicate the protective role assumed by men in past environments; it could be the result of food-gathering specialisation whereby men hunted and women gathered; or it could reflect male competition for females in uni-male or multi-male groups. The dimorphism for humans is mild, however, compared to that for gorillas; this would indicate that *Homo sapiens* did not evolve in a system of uni-male harem mating characteristic of gorillas, for if they had men would be much larger. Moreover, if early human males did routinely compete for access to

Table 4.1 Physical characteristics of the great apes in relation to mating and reproduction

Species	Male body weight (kg)	Female body weight (kg)	Dimorphism M/F	Mating system	Weight of testes (g)	Weight of testes as % of body weight	Approx. number of sperm per ejaculate (× 10⁷)
Humans (*Homo sapiens*)	70	63	1.1	Monogamy and Polygyny?	25–50	0.04–0.08	25
Common chimps (*Pan troglodytes*)	40	30	1.3	Multi-male in promiscuous groups	120	0.3	60
Orang-utan (*Pongo pygmaeus*)	84	38	2.2	Uni-male Temporary liaisons	35	0.05	7
Gorilla (*Gorilla gorilla*)	160	89	1.8	Uni-male Polygyny	30	0.02	5

Adapted from Cartwright (2000). Data from various sources: Harcourt *et al.* (1981), Foley (1989), Warner *et al.* (1974).

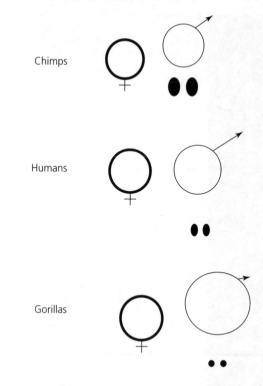

Figure 4.4 **Female's view of males illustrating relative size of body, penis and testes (adapted from Short, 1994)**

The size of the circle for each male compared to the female indicates body size dimorphism for the species. The size of the pair of solid circles indicates size of testes relative to other males of each species. The crosses show the relative size of female genitalia at oestrus. The size of the arrows indicates relative penis size for males. The large size of the human penis compared to other primates remains a mystery

groups of females, we would not only expect a higher level of body size dimorphism but also smaller testes. Notice how the testes of gorillas relative to body size are less than half the average for humans. On the other hand, if early humans had behaved like chimpanzees in multi-male groups then we would expect larger testes since females would mate with many males and this would drive up the size of testes in males to enable them to compete effectively. A simple calculation shows that if human males had the same relative size of testes as chimps they would roughly be as large as tennis balls.

In Figure 4.4 the data from Table 4.1 is summarised by showing in a schematic form how male humans, gorillas, orang-utans and chimps appear from a female perspective. The size of the large circle relative to the female shows the degree of sexual dimorphism in the species. The length of the arrows and the pair of dark shapes show the relative size of the penises and testes of the males. One enigmatic feature of male morphology is the large size of the human penis. If humans did not evolve in multi-male groups like those of chimpanzees then we would expect the male penis to be smaller, relatively speaking, than that of the male chimp. This is a puzzle awaiting explanation.

From a comparison of human testis size with other primates, Short concludes that we are not 'inherently monogamous . . . neither are we adapted to a multimale promiscuous mating system'; his view is that 'we are basically a polygynous primate in which the polygyny usually takes the form of serial monogamy' (Short, 1994, p. 13). More recent evidence (see Birkhead, 2000) suggests that females are not as naturally monogamous as some men might wish. The size of men's testicles and the large number of sperm produced suggest that sperm competition has been a feature of our evolutionary ancestry. Now it takes two to tango, so if sperm compete then a woman must have mated with more than one man.

Examine the data from Table 4.1 on the number of sperm produced per ejaculate. Discuss the significance of differences between the different species in terms of sperm competition theory and mating behaviour.

Progress exercise

Many enigmas about human mating remain, but one consistent message from physical anthropology is perhaps that humans are nearly but not quite monogamous. If males can accumulate enough wealth they will practise opportunistic polygyny, either serially or simultaneously. Meanwhile, the continuous sexual receptivity of women enforces a strong bond between herself and her partner, but likewise enables a spot of polyandry if appropriate. A shorthand description of typical human mating might be an ostensibly monogamous system plagued by adultery. Not so different, if we are honest with ourselves, to what we suspected all along.

Evidence that both males and females make considerable investment in a relationship comes from the fact that both sexes have a highly refined sense of sexual attractiveness. We do not mate at random – we choose our partners carefully. Coupled with this there is strong agreement on what features are attractive in males and females. Choosing our mates and the criteria we apply in this process are the subjects of the next section.

Evolution and sexual desire: some expectations and approaches

Darwinian psychology views attractiveness in terms of reproductive fitness. Features that are positive indicators of reproductive fitness in a potential mate should be viewed as attractive by males and females. In this sense, beauty is more than skin deep – it is to be found in the 'eye' of the genes.

Of all the features used in appraising a potential mate two in particular have produced robust empirical findings that reveal inherent differences between male and female taste. They are physical attractiveness and the status of males. In the case of male status, the application of the principles established earlier predicts that, since females make a heavy investment in raising young, and since the care of both parents is needed following birth, females will be attracted to males who show signs of being able to bring resources to the relationship. This follows from the fact that the best way for a woman to secure reproductive success is to ensure that the relatively few children she is able to raise in a lifetime receive adequate care.

If females respond to indicators of potential provisioning and status then males should be attracted to females that appear fertile and physically capable of caring for children. Since the period of female fertility (roughly 13–45) occupies a narrower age band than that of the male (13–65) we would also expect the age of prospective partners to be evaluated differently by each sex. Men should be fussier about age than women and hence rate physical features that correlate with youth and fertility higher on a scale of importance than women.

To test these expectations we can examine human preferences using data from at least two sources:

1. What people say about their desires in response to questionnaires;
2. What people look for when they advertise for a partner.

Cross-cultural comparisons using questionnaires

The use of questionnaires to establish fundamental patterns in human sexual desire obviously faces a number of problems. Participants may not be honest in their replies; there may be bias in that people with specific tastes may be more or less likely to reply; and, perhaps most seriously, any patterns observed in one culture may reflect cultural practices and the norms of socialisation rather than universal constants of human nature. In an effort to circumvent this latter problem, David Buss (1989) conducted a questionnaire survey of men and women in 37 different cultures across Africa, Europe, North American Oceania and South America, and hence across a wide diversity of religious, ethnic, racial and economic groups. Buss's work remains one of the most thorough attempts so far to examine the sensitivity of expressed mating preferences to cultural variation and to relate sexual preferences to an evolutionary framework. From the general considerations noted above, Buss tested several hypotheses (Table 4.2).

The results in terms of the number of cultures where there was a significant ($p < 0.05$) difference between the qualities examined in each hypothesis above are shown in Table 4.3.

There are clearly problems with many studies based on questionnaires, particularly when unrepresentative samples are used. One sometimes gets the impression that in America, where Darwinian psychology is taught in many universities, undergraduates are constantly being plagued by interviewees asking about their sex lives. The type of people willing to reveal information about their behaviour and desires may not be typical of the whole population. It could also be that people give the answers that they expect are correct and appropriate for a given culture. Nevertheless, the findings tend to be in agreement with evolutionary expectations.

One thing to remind ourselves of in considering such work is that there is a great deal of agreement between men and women over what characteristics they desire in a potential partner. In Buss's survey, both sexes listed intelligence, personality, looks and religious views as important. What Buss did was to tease out what differences there are in our tastes; and these differences he found consistent with evolutionary theory.

Table 4.2 Predictions on mate choice preferences tested cross-culturally by Buss (1989)

Prediction	Adaptive significance in relation to reproductive success
Women should value earning potential in a mate more highly than should men	The likelihood of a woman's offspring surviving and their subsequent health can be increased by allocation of resources to the woman and her children
Men should value physical attractiveness more highly than should women	The fitness and reproductive potential of a female are more heavily influenced by age than for a man. Attractiveness is a strong indicator of age and fertility
Men, on the whole, are likely to prefer women younger than themselves	Men reach sexual maturity later than women do. Also as above
Men will value chastity more so than women will	'Mom's babies, daddy's maybes'. For a male to have raised a child not his own would have been, and still is, highly damaging to his reproductive fitness
Women should rate ambition and drive in a prospective partner more highly than men do in their partners	Ambition and drive are linked to the ability to secure resources and offer protection, both of which would be fitness enhancing to a woman

Table 4.3 Number of cultures supporting or otherwise hypotheses on gender differences in mate preference

Hypothesis	Number of cultures supporting hypothesis	Number of cultures contrary (con) to hypothesis or result not significant (ns)
	Percentage of total in parentheses	*Percentage of total in parentheses*
Women value earning potential greater than men	36 (97%)	1 ns (3%)
Men value physical attributes more than women	34 (92%)	3 ns (8%)
Women value ambition and industriousness more than men	29 (78%)	3 con (8%) 5 ns (13%)
Men value chastity more than women	23 (62%)	14 ns (38%)
Men prefer women younger than themselves	37 (100%)	0 (0%)
Data from Buss (1989).		

Surveys using published advertisements

An intriguing way to gather information on mating preferences is to inspect the content of 'lonely hearts' advertisements in the personal column of newspapers and magazines. A typical advertisement is shown in Figure 4.5.

Notice that the advertisement offers information about the advertiser as well as his preferences for a mate. Gathering such information is less intrusive than using questionnaires and less subject to the well-known phenomenon that interviewees will tend to comply with what they take to be the expectations of the questioner. Moreover, the data is 'serious' in that it represents actual attempts of people to secure partners.

> Single prof. male, 30, graduate, tall, non-smoker, own home, good sense of humour, seeks younger slim woman for friendship and maybe something more.

Figure 4.5 **Typical 'lonely hearts' advertisement**

Progress exercise

Analysis of advertisements

Examine the ad shown below.

Q1. Break down its components into (a) what is offered, (b) what is sought.

> Petite slim 20 something woman seeks professional male or businessman for outings and romance. Must be graduate with good sense of humour and love of the arts.

Q2. Suppose you were now to undertake a survey of advertisements in your local paper. By now you understand the theory (hopefully) and know what differences are expected between the tastes of men and women. How could you control for your own bias in deciding what an advert is offering and seeking?

Greenlees and McGrew (1994) examined 1599 such advertisements in the columns of *Private Eye*. The results for physical appearance and financial security are shown in Figure 4.6.

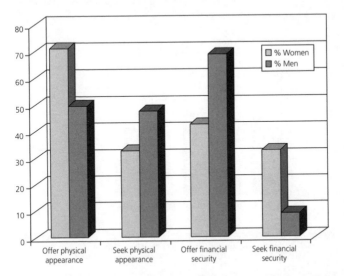

Figure 4.6 **Percentage of advertisers seeking and offering physical appearance and financial security according to gender. Data from *Ethology and Sociobiology* 15, Greenlees, I.A. and McGrew, W.C., Sex and age differences in preferences and tactics of mate attraction: analysis of published advertisements, 59–72, copyright 1994, with permission from Elsevier Science**

The results shown in Figure 4.6 are consistent with the questionnaire surveys of Buss discussed earlier and they support the following hypotheses:

1. Women more than men look for indications of financial security.
2. Men more than women offer financial security.
3. Women more than men advertise their physical appearance.
4. Men more than women seek indications of physical appearance.

Progress exercise

The work of Greenlees and McGrew has been repeated many times with similar findings. Figure 4.7 shows details from a survey by Dunbar (1995) showing how the propensity to seek resources in a personal advertisement varies with age.

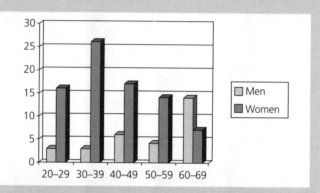

Figure 4.7 **Percentage of advertisers in personal columns seeking resources (modified from Dunbar, 1995)**

Q1. Suggest a hypothesis that could explain why the difference between men and women varies with the age group.

Q2. Suggest a way in which you could test your hypothesis.

Facial attractiveness

Faces carry a mass of information and, unsurprisingly, humans are extremely responsive to each other's faces. Eibl-Eibesfeldt proposed that qualities that men find attractive in the faces of women correspond to 'infantile' features such as a small, upturned nose, large eyes and small chin. Such features are found in young children and it may be that women have developed these features to evoke the caring response that males feel towards their offspring. In effect, women's faces have evolved to exploit the perceptual bias in male brains (Eibl-Eibesfeldt, 1989). At the anecdotal level there was a hit pop song of the 1960s containing the refrain 'Baby face, you've got that cutest little baby face'

– not one of the greatest achievements of modern music but revealing nevertheless. Other features in women's faces that men find attractive tend to be associated with signs of youth and fertility. As women age, increasing levels of testosterone stimulate hair growth. Significantly, men tend to find hairless faces in women more attractive – as evidenced by the efforts of women to remove facial hair. Hair colour also tends to darken with age and the attractiveness of blonde hair could be that it is a reliable sign of youth.

The faces of people differ enormously and humans are especially attentive to the faces of each other. Given this wide divergence in the shape and attractiveness of faces, an interesting question to pursue is what the average face would look like. Since the number of very attractive people in a population is rather small one might expect that the average face is far from attractive; extremes are usually a long way off from the mean or the mode. It was Galton, Darwin's cousin, who first investigated this in the nineteenth century. He used newly invented techniques in photography to superimpose many images of faces on top of one another. The result then is a composite face that can be regarded as a rather fuzzy indication of what the average would look like. Surprisingly, the result he found was that average faces appear rather attractive.

Galton's work has been repeated on numerous occasions, and although some work indicates that really attractive faces are not perfect averages the general thrust of his work has been supported. Using a computerised technique of merging faces, Langlois and Roggman found that not only were composite faces more attractive than individual ones, but the more faces that went into making a composite the more attractive, up to a point, the face became. A face composed of 32 faces, for example, was more attractive than one composed of two faces (Langlois and Roggman, 1990). Symons suggested in 1979 that the average was rated as attractive because the average of any trait would tend to be optimally adapted for any trait, since the mean of a distribution presumably represents the best solution to the adaptive problem (Symons, 1979).

To understand this point, consider the analogy with height. Most humans tend to fall somewhere between 5 feet and just over 6 feet tall. The mean height of people in the West has increased slightly over the last few hundred years, but this is a response to better diet rather than any evolutionary change. With regard to height is it fair to say that natural selection has exerted a stabilising influence. Humans are now about the right height to cope with the survival problems of the ecological niche in which we evolved about 100,000 years ago. If we were any smaller, then the threat from predators would have increased and we may have lacked the body strength to hunt and obtain food. If we were any larger then injuries when we fell over would have been more serious; additionally, we would have to obtain more food to support more body mass. We can say that our height is an optimum adaptation to the environment in which we evolved. If this is the case then the average is just about right and probably the best height to be. From this it follows that if we have evolved to view well-adapted people as desirable (from a genetic point of view) then the average should be regarded as attractive.

Another possibility is that average faces are highly symmetrical. This follows from the fact that although each one of us has asymmetrical features, taking an average tends to iron out these differences. Why symmetry should be rated as attractive is understandable when we realise that infection by parasites – which must have been a constant problem for our ancestors, as it still is for some people of the world today – tends to decrease symmetry. So if you are looking for a partner who is parasite free and has a genome that has given them a good immune system to resist parasites – a genome that would, therefore, be a good one to pool with your own – then symmetry is a good yardstick by which to measure them.

In testing these ideas the experimental problem to overcome is that there are at least two variables: averageness and symmetry. Perret and co-workers at the University of St Andrews used computer techniques to alter the symmetry of facial images and then investigated rating of attractiveness. He found that as the symmetry of a face increases so did its attractiveness rating (Perrett *et al.*, 1999).

Sexual jealousy

Shakespeare referred to sexual jealousy as the 'green-eyed monster' and without doubt it is one of the fiercest emotions that humans can experience. Darwinian psychology would predict that jealousy is a sexually dimorphic emotion, meaning that it will be experienced differently by each sex. In males it is likely that the emotion of jealousy is an adaptive response to the risk that past and future parental investment may be 'wasted' on offspring from another male. This is the essential male predicament that lies at the heart of human sexual relations: before the modern era with the advent of DNA testing, males could rarely be 100% certain of their paternity. Females, in contrast, despite the few cases of mislabelling in modern hospitals, are virtually assured that they are the mother of a child – it is hard not to know that you have just given birth. On this basis we can draw up a table of how we can expect jealousy to be distributed in form and intensity between males and females (Table 4.4).

Table 4.4 **Predicted differences in the experience of jealousy by men and women**

Men	Women
Should be particularly concerned about physical infidelity. Raising children that are not his own is a waste of effort from a genetic point of view	Should be more concerned about emotional infidelity. The prospect that a man may withdraw his support and resources is damaging to the reproductive fitness of a woman
The emotion of jealousy should be more strongly experienced by men than women as a result of the need to ensure paternity	The emotion will be strong but confidence in maternity would predict it to be more weakly experienced in women than in men
Men are predicted to undertake measures to increase paternity confidence and control the sexuality of their partners	

To test for sexual differences in the experience of jealousy, Buss *et al.* (1992) issued questionnaires to undergraduates at the University of Michigan, asking them to rank the level of distress caused by either the sexual or emotional infidelity of a partner. The result suggested that men tend to be more concerned about sexual infidelity and women more about emotional infidelity.

The same effect was observed when subjects were 'wired up' and tested for physiological responses to the suggestion that they imagine their partner behaving unfaithfully either sexually or emotionally. The difference was less marked for women but men consistently and significantly showed heightened distress to thoughts of sexual infidelity compared to emotional.

The prediction on the control of sexuality can be illustrated qualitatively by an examination of some of the cultural practices that seem to be designed to control the sexuality of women. These include the following:

1. *Veiling, chaperoning, purdah and incarceration*
   Obscuring a woman's body and her facial features, ensuring she is always accompanied when she travels and restricting her freedom to travel and make social contacts, are common practices in patriarchal societies and can be seen as ways of restricting the sexual access of women to other men. Significantly, it is usually only practised on women of reproductive age; children and post-menopausal women are excluded.

2. *Genital mutilation*
   Unlike male circumcision, female genital mutilation is specifically designed to reduce the sexual activity of the victim. Practices range from partial or complete clitoridectomy to infibulation. Girls aged 13–18 of the Sabiny tribe in Uganda are taken to a village clearing where their clitorises are removed. It is estimated that about 6000 girls are mutilated in this way each day in Africa and that more than 65 million women and girls now alive in Africa have been 'circumcised' (Hosken, 1979). The practice is condemned by some governments, including the Ugandan, but the Sabiny women resent attempts to ban the practice as cultural interference.

3. *Double standards in social mores and laws*
   Until relatively recently British culture was riddled with examples of double standards in sexual morality. There were, for example, far more derogatory labels for promiscuous women than for promiscuous men. In Victorian times a woman was said to be 'ruined' if she had intercourse before marriage. Such a term was never applied to men. Instead, epithets such as 'dashing blade' were

applied to men with many sexual conquests. Even the law reflected this. Until recent reforms (the last 30 years), for example, laws in the UK tended to define adultery in terms of the marital status of the woman. The marital status of the man was usually ignored. Similarly, if a wife was adulterous it represented clear grounds for divorce; if a husband was adulterous divorce was a rarer consequence. In addition, as late as 1973 Englishmen could legally restrain wives who were intent on leaving them.

Darwinian psychology and divorce

Divorce statistics provide a convenient testing ground for a number of hypotheses about human mating. Examine Figure 4.8, which gives details of the number of divorces granted in England and Wales for 1995 broken down by the sex of the party to whom divorce was granted and the reason given. The term behaviour means that one or the other sex was violent, abusive or mistreated the other partner or the children. To understand the figure the bars for men, for example, indicate that in 1995 about 16,000 men were granted a divorce on the grounds that their wives had committed adultery, and about 11,000 granted divorce on the grounds that their wives were behaving badly.

Progress exercise

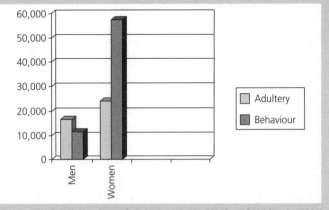

Figure 4.8 **Total number of divorces in England and Wales in 1995 broken down by sex of petitioning party and reasons of adultery or bad behaviours. Source of data: Office of Population Censuses and Surveys**

Q1. Suggest an explanation in terms of Darwinian psychology for the pattern observed in Figure 4.8.

Figure 4.9 shows the percentage of all divorces in any age group according to sex and age. To read this graph you read that, for example, in the 20–24-year age group 88% of all divorces were granted to the wife and 12% to the husband.

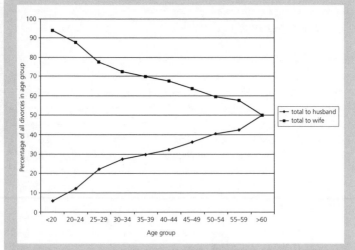

Figure 4.9 **Percentage of divorces in each age group according to sex and age group for England and Wales, 1995. Source of data: Office of Population Census and Surveys**

Q2.

(a) Describe the pattern observed.

(b) Offer an analysis of the data in terms of Darwinian psychology. (Hint: you may like to consider the shorter period of biological fertility of women compared to men).

Figure 4.10 shows how the importance of adultery as a reason for petitioning for divorce changes with the age group. The percentage figures are percentages of the sex in that age group granted divorce. Thus for the age group 20–24 years, 45% of the divorces awarded to men in this age group were due to men complaining about adultery.

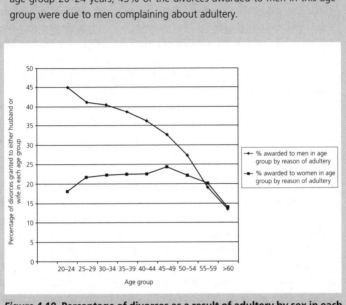

Figure 4.10 **Percentage of divorces as a result of adultery by sex in each age group. Source of data: Office of Population Censuses and Surveys**

Q3. Comment on the pattern observed in the light of evolutionary theory.

In this chapter, we have examined the emotion of sexual jealousy. Such an emotion is part of our psychological make-up and difficult to avoid at some time in our life. This brings us to the subject of whether emotions that we experience are roughly the same for all people or whether the categories of our emotional life are products of our culture and upbringing. If emotions are universal, so that, for example, sexual jealousy is an emotion found in all cultures, and potentially in nearly all humans, we can then profitably inquire as to what adaptive significance emotions have. This is one of the topics of the next chapter.

Summary

- Between men and women there is a mild degree of sexual dimorphism in body size. This is consistent with a human ancestry where males competed with other males for access to females. The dimorphism is smaller than would be expected, however, had humans evolved in uni-male polygynous groups (i.e. harem-like situations) such as characterise gorilla societies.

- The size of men's testes compared to those of chimps and gorillas suggests that we did not evolve in 'promiscuous' multi-male, multi-female groups, nor did we practise polygynous mating to any marked degree. The evidence suggests that early humans practised a mixture of monogamy and mild polygamy.

- Men and women make different investments in offspring and can be expected to employ different criteria when choosing a mate. Men value youth and attractiveness more highly than do women. Women value status and resources in a partner more highly than do men.

- Men and women can be expected to experience and respond to the emotion of jealousy in different ways. Women are predicted to be more concerned about emotional infidelity and withdrawal of support than are men. Men are predicted to be more worried about physical infidelity. There is some empirical support for these predictions.

Review exercise

Fill in the blanks with the terms below.

Differences in body size between males and females are part of a phenomenon called _____ . The sex that is the larger of the two can be expected to compete for the smaller sex. This process of intrasexual selection is usually found when mating is _____ . The fact that human males are slightly larger than females could indicate that males once competed for females. The testes of men are much larger, however, than those of _____ and this is consistent with the suggestion that humans did not evolve in groups consisting of a single male having exclusive sexual access to a harem of females.

For men _____ is an ever-present problem and they have evolved psychological mechanisms to increase paternity confidence. One of these might be the experience of the emotion of _____ . Men experience a longer period of _____ than women and can be expected to be preferentially attracted to _____ women. Women are predicted to be less concerned about age than men but to look for signs of _____ in a potential partner.

Terms: (only eight of these terms can be correctly used): *polygamous, jealousy, paternity confidence, younger, sexual dimorphism, status and wealth, gorillas, chimps, sperm competition, monogamous, menopause, fertility, older*

Further reading

Betzig, L. (ed.) (1997). *Human Nature: A Critical Reader*. Oxford: Oxford University Press. A useful book that contains numerous original articles on human sexuality together with a critique in retrospect by the original authors.

Short, R. and Potts, M. (1999). *Ever Since Adam and Eve: The Evolution of Human Sexuality*. Cambridge, UK: University Press. Superbly illustrated and authoritative work. A humane account of the evolution and significance of human sexuality.

Archetypes of the psyche: fears and anxieties as adaptive responses

◈ The universality of emotional life
◈ Mental health and archetypes of the psyche
◈ Fears, anxieties and phobias
◈ Summary

The universality of emotional life

Humans have a finely developed repertoire of emotional responses, and, although our experiences are intensely personal, we can share our emotions with, and recognise the emotional states of, fellow humans. However, if we take a cross-cultural perspective, are the ways in which we express our emotions with gestures and facial expressions, and recognise them accordingly, universal or culturally determined? Put simply, is a smile a smile in any part of the world or are there cultures where a smile might mean 'I am angry' or 'I am sad'? In answer to this we must note that there is now abundant evidence that the forms in which we express our emotions are universal features of human nature.

Testing for the universality and instinctive nature of emotional expression and experience poses numerous experimental problems for the evolutionary psychologist. One is to disentangle the effects on people of mass culture, with its supply of ready-made images of emotions and their expression, from what might naturally develop. To overcome this, Paul Ekman in the 1960s went about interviewing and testing people in a wide variety of cultures. He showed photographs of people's faces in various emotional states to subjects in Chile, Argentina, Brazil, the USA and Japan and asked his subjects to attach a label – anger, happiness, surprise, fear, sadness and disgust – to each picture. Later, such studies were extended by Ekman and others to include a total of 21 countries. The results were highly significant: despite the numerous differences between such cultures in terms of economic development and religious values, there was overwhelming agreement about faces that showed happiness, sadness and disgust (Ekman, 1973).

Ekman then applied similar tests to the South Fore people in Papua New Guinea. At the time these people were still living a Stone Age lifestyle without a written language and impervious to the global reach of Western culture. Ekman cleverly overcame the language barrier to obtain decisive results. The South Fore people chose the same facial expression for their emotions as those in the previous 21 countries sampled.

From such studies it increasingly begins to look as if our emotional life (at least in the way it is expressed facially) is part of a standard development programme. Since this programme develops consistently in all cultures, it would seem reasonable to suppose that it has been shaped by natural selection. Once this is established we can begin to ask questions about the adaptive value of having emotions and expressing them.

A plausible start might be to see emotions as acting like other physiological responses such as pain, hunger and sexual arousal. With these it is easy to see how they function to ensure that the organism avoids danger, thrives and sexually reproduces. In this light emotions regulate our behaviour to ensure that our genes survive. This is the point made by Nesse and Williams in their influential book *Evolution and Healing*:

Just as the capacity for experiencing fatigue has evolved to protect us from overexertion, the capacity for sadness may have evolved to prevent additional losses. (Nesse and Williams, 1995, p. 209)

In other words, when we are hopelessly losing it is best to quit and sadness provides the trigger. Without this insight, both sadness and depression would appear to be counter-productive since they are emotional states that lead us to withdraw from normal life and its opportunities to increase our fitness. Both these emotions, following as they do the loss of something valuable to our interests such as power, status, resources or a close friend or mate, lead us to stop our current activities, reflect on our actions and doubt the wisdom of our recent strategies. In this sense depression is akin to pain that makes us stop eating unripe fruit or stop prodding that wasps' nest. When you are in a hole stop digging, as the saying goes.

Mental health and archetypes of the psyche

In the light of Darwinian psychology, mental health can be seen as the proper functioning of an adaptive emotional system. In support of this view, the psychiatrists Anthony Steven and John Price propose five laws of psychodynamics describing the way the human mind develops as a result of inherent and environmental factors (Stevens and Price, 1996):

1. Whenever a behavioural disposition is to be found in all cultures it is the expression of an innate propensity or archetype. In this context, an archetype is a pattern of development that is common to all normally functioning humans and represents something laid down by natural selection early in our evolution.
2. Archetypes possess an inherent dynamic to express themselves.
3. Mental health is the expression and fulfilment of the goals of the archetypes.
4. Psychopathology results from the frustration of archetypal goals.
5. Psychiatric symptoms are the extreme and exaggerated expression of adaptive responses.

Ideas concerning archetypes and the expression of innate drives are, of course, not new ones, and both notions can be found in Freud and Jung. But whereas Jung interpreted archetypes in terms of his mystical collective unconscious, and Freud over-stressed the frustration of archetypal intent in childhood (and was, besides, a **Lamarckian**), modern evolutionary psychiatry of the sort advanced by Stevens and Price is more securely based on Darwinian principles.

The term 'archetype' is consistent with the **modular** view of the mind found in the works of the American evolutionary psychologists

John Tooby and Leda Cosmides. They adopt the premise that the mind is what the brain does. The brain, in their view, is not a formless mass waiting to be structured by experience after birth, nor is it a general problem-solving 'on-board computer'; rather, they regard it as best interpreted as consisting of a whole series of problem-solving modules. They use the analogy of a Swiss army knife that unfolds to reveal an array of useful tools, all of which to some degree are independent.

We should not take this analogy too far though: the mental modules of the brain are almost certainly not so independent as indicated by this analogy. There are, for example, plenty of well-documented cases of people regaining a function after damage to one part of the brain by learning to use other areas for similar tasks. In the view of Tooby and Cosmides these mental tools or modules have been shaped by natural selection to solve the problems humans encountered in the EEA. Some of these modules may be mechanisms for:

- recognition of kin and non-kin;
- choosing a suitable mate;
- language acquisition;
- recognition of a group and an out-group;
- detection of cheating.

The possession of the above mechanisms would have been vital for the survival and propagation of hominid genes during our evolution. If these views about the evolutionary origin of modules and archetypes are correct then it may be fruitful to look at their functioning and malfunctioning in terms of evolutionary theory. This opens the way to a Darwinian understanding of mental disorders. Before moving to these extreme conditions, however, it may be worth examining the fears and anxieties that we all experience from time to time. This is considered below.

Fears, anxieties and phobias

Anxiety is often useful. A bit of anxiety before an exam, for example, may persuade you to revise more thoroughly. Anxiety in the face of danger, such as walking through a field with a bull inside, may ensure you keep your distance or, more sensibly, avoid the field altogether. In general terms, showing fear in the face of a hazard may persuade you to change your course of action and reduce your risk by taking more caution. We should at this point distinguish between fears and phobias. Fears are natural human emotions that bear some relationship to the source of danger. Phobias are fears wildly out of proportion to the actual hazards faced. Fears are adaptive whereas phobias can lead to maladaptive behaviour.

Fears can assist survival in a number of ways:

- By stimulating evolved physiological reactions such as the release of nonadrenaline (epinephrine). This hormone acts on blood receptors to aid clotting should a wound be received; it also stimulates the heart, causing blood to flow faster and the liver to release glucose, both of which result in more energy available to tissues for flight or fight.
- Cessation of movement. Fear sometimes freezes people on the spot. This is not a wise reaction if a bull elephant is charging you but in many contexts is a sensible response. Not moving helps concealment from a predator; it may be that you have not been seen and running away would attract attention.
- Flight and submission. In many cases running away is the best response. As an alternative, fear could bow us into submission to a more dominant member of our species, thereby avoiding aggression.

If fear and moderate anxiety represent evolved responses then it could be that more specific manifestations represent ancestral memories of hazards encountered in the history of our ancestors. Fear of the dark, for example, is clearly understandable in these terms: humans are vulnerable at night from attack by predators with better night vision or from humans with ill-intent. It has even been suggested that the function of sleep relates to vulnerability of humans at night. If there are risks attached to moving about, making a noise and not functioning very effectively then it is better to shut up shop, keep still and remain dormant until it is light again. Sleep is the way in which genes ensure that their vehicle (the human body) avoids risky behaviour. Table 5.1 shows how we could, in principle, map specific fears to the adaptive memory they represent.

The fears shown in Table 5.1 are ingrained to some degree in the human psyche. It is significant that more city dwellers go to psychiatrists with excessive fears of snakes and strangers than do those

Figure 5.1 The Scream **from a lithograph by Edvard Munch (1863–1944) made in 1895. © Munch Museum/Munch–Ellingsen Group, BONO, Oslo, DACS, London 2001**

The Scream is a powerful portrayal of the angst and alienation many people feel sometimes in their life. Although he lived to be 81, Munch himself suffered from a number of anxieties. He felt a dread when he had to cross an open square and like Van Gogh and Gauguin was convinced that he was persecuted by others. He suffered a complete nervous breakdown in 1908 and spent 6 months in a clinic in Copenhagen

Table 5.1 Types of fear and their adaptive origins	
Type of fear	*Adaptive origin*
Fear of snakes	Poisonous snakes have been a threat to primates and hominids for the last few million years
Fear of heights (acrophobia)	Humans are relatively large animals and falling has always posed a grave danger. Significantly, acrophobia usually provokes a freezing reaction, making it less likely that a person will fall
Claustrophobia	In a small confined space humans are vulnerable since escape is difficult
Stranger anxiety (xenophobia)	Harm from unfamiliar humans, especially males. Response to threat of disease transmission – strangers could bring diseases from remote areas to which the local population has not evolved a defence
Agoraphobia	Risks lie beyond the familiar territory of the home

with fears of cars or electrical sockets (Buss, 1999). Yet for modern urban humans, electricity and cars represent statistically a far greater risk than snakes or strangers.

The fear that children often show before strangers is understandable in these terms. It is likely that infanticide represented a real risk for our primate ancestors. In polygynous mating groups of several animal species, when the dominant male is displaced by another, the new male sets about killing the infants by his previous rival. This has the effect of bringing the females back into oestrus and also ensuring that neither he nor his mates waste energy on raising infants that are not his own. This brutal side of our past may have left its mark on modern humans. The evolutionary psychologists Margo Wilson and Martin Daly have found that the risk of infanticide for a stepchild is 100 times higher than for a child with natural parents (Daly and Wilson, 1988). It is perhaps not surprising then that infant humans are often afraid of strangers. The fearful and often tearful reaction of a 1-year-old child when a strange male approaches may be a relic of our brutal past. In fact such a reaction has been documented in a number of cultures (Smith, 1979).

Progress exercise

This activity is a thought experiment that invites you to think about humans in a selectionist way. Imagine that our ancestors on the African plains some 500,000 years ago encountered two types of fruit. The first fruit (A) contained substances that promoted fertility: it increased the rate of sperm production and increased sexual arousal. The second (B) depressed fertility, reduced the sex drive and gradually made men infertile. Speculate on what the reaction of modern humans (before they knew intellectually what the properties of the fruits were) would be to these fruits in terms of their taste and their appeal.

Study the lithograph by Munch called *Anxiety* shown in Figure 5.2. Describe the way in which the artist conveys the emotion of anxiety.

Figure 5.2 Anxiety by Munch (1896). Munch Museum/Munch–Ellingsen Group, BONO, Oslo, DACS, London 2001

Summary

- There is increasing evidence that the forms of emotional expression are the same the world over. All humans seem to share a standard emotional package. Although the events that spark off emotions will vary from culture to culture, we are all capable of recognising the signs of grief, joy, anger, sadness and other basic emotions in other members of our species irrespective of their race or culture.

• A fruitful view of emotions is that they represent ingrained and to some degree genetically determined responses. They are common to all humans and have been shaped by natural selection to serve some adaptive function to assist the human organism to thrive and reproduce.

• Fear and anxiety are part of the human package and they usually serve us well by directing our actions to reduce risks or improve performance.

Review exercise

The table below shows a set of commonly experienced emotions. In the right-hand column try to offer an account of what adaptive purpose having such emotions serves.

Emotion	Possible function
Sexual jealousy	
Fear of water	
Delight in the behaviour of young infants	
Laughter when someone has made a particularly clever joke	
Guilt in not returning a favour or helping a friend	
Disgust at the sight of, say, drinking water contaminated with faecal matter	

Further reading

There are very few books addressed to students below undergraduate level on the evolutionary approach to mental disorders, but the following texts may be accessible.

Baron-Cohen, S. (1997). *The Maladapted Mind*. Hove, UK: Psychology Press. See the Preface and Chapters 1, 4 and 12.

Nesse, R.M. and Williams, G.C. (1995). *Evolution and Healing*. London: Weidenfeld & Nicolson. A readable survey of the whole topic of what is sometimes called Darwinian medicine. Chapters 1, 2 and 14 are the most useful for this chapter.

Stearns, S.C. (ed.) (1999). *Evolution in Health and Disease*. Oxford: Oxford University Press. A book based on a high-level conference held in Switzerland in 1997. It reports on some interesting research findings. The most suitable chapters for this section are 1, 8 and 23.

Stevens, A. and Price, J. (1996). *Evolutionary Psychiatry*. London: Routledge. One of the few books dealing solely with this topic. It should be accessible to the good A-level candidate. See Chapters 1, 2, 3, 5, 8 and 13.

Evolutionary explanations of mental disorders

Mental disorders: problems of terminology
Mental abnormalities: some hypotheses
A genetic basis for mental disorders
The adaptive value of genetically based disorders
Evolutionary psychiatry: prospects
Summary

Mental disorders: problems of terminology

In the previous chapter, we saw how emotions that we find distressing, such as sadness, fear and anxiety, may be responses that are, or at least once were, useful to us. Like pain and grief they are the price of the entry ticket to the human race; and, however unpleasant they may be, they are part of our psychological make-up. Nevertheless, we still have a lot of explaining to do since clearly, in some people, we find responses so extreme, irrational and self-destructive that they must be disorders.

Defining a mental disorder is not as easy as it might sound. Traditional definitions of abnormal behaviour usually use criteria such as statistical infrequency, deviations from what would normally be expected from the individual, behaviour that violates moral standards of a culture, and behaviour that causes distress to the sufferer. However, all of these criteria have their problems. To take two examples, the moral standards of a culture may themselves be questionable; also, many behaviours that lie at the extreme ends of a normal distribution, such as high intelligence, creativity or sporting skill, are not usually thought of as abnormal.

In Britain and America, one of the most commonly used manuals of criteria for abnormal behaviour is the *Diagnostic and Statistical Manual of Mental Disorders* (DSM), published by the American Psychiatric Association. This manual places particular emphasis on the extent of personal suffering experienced by the victim and the impairment of normal life that this causes.

The evolutionary psychologist David Buss criticises traditional definitions of disorders as being too subjective for scientific clarity. Buss has argued that evolutionary psychology provides a clear criterion for identifying a mental dysfunction: 'Dysfunction occurs when the mechanism is not performing as it was designed to perform in the contexts in which it was designed to perform' (Buss, 1999, p. 399). This is helpful but does not remove all the problems. We still have to ascertain what mechanisms we have and what they were designed to do. In addition, genetic variability will ensure that people will differ in the characteristics of their mechanisms and in the efficiency of their performance; unless, that is, genetic variability in these features is exhausted and all humans are roughly the same. Buss suggests that, using the definition above, evolved mechanisms can fail in three distinct ways:

1. The mechanism fails to become activated when the appropriate problem is confronted.
2. The mechanism is activated in inappropriate contexts, e.g. sexual desire for close relatives or young children.
3. The mechanism fails to coordinate properly with other mechanisms.

Buss argues that each of these types of failure could be caused by chance genetic variation (such as genetic defects following mutations), or developmental insults (e.g. damage to the brain) or a combination of these.

The American evolutionary philosophers Murphy and Stich (2000) have also expressed dissatisfaction with the DSM approach. They argue that this classification of mental disorders takes no account of the underlying mental structures or design features of the brain:

the DSM approach to classification is not guided by any theory about the structure and functioning of normal minds and makes no attempt to uncover and use facts about the underlying psychological, biological and environmental mechanisms and processes that give rise to symptoms. (Murphy and Stich, 2000, p. 69)

To illustrate this point we can consider the analogy of a television monitor. A TV is a highly designed and intricate piece of equipment. Most people probably have a limited understanding of how the system works and how the different components interact and feed information to other components. If the TV malfunctions and, for example, no picture is seen we might classify this as a picture deficit disorder. Yet there could be many root causes of this problem that are not really conveyed by lumping them together under one set of symptoms. It could be a power failure, a fuse failure in the plug or socket, a broken contact in the TV or a complete breakdown of the cathode ray tube, etc. These authors call for a new approach to the classification of mental disorders based on basic science.

The fact that evolution has provided us with an emotional system that, by and large, regulates our behaviour towards our best reproductive interests does not mean that the system will always function perfectly. By analogy, the human immune system is a wonderful piece of physiological precision engineering sculpted by hard-fought battles with parasites and disease over millions of years. For most of us, most of the time, it does a sterling job of keeping infections and disease at bay. Yet, for some people it is prone to malfunctioning. It can become too active and attack the body's own tissues, causing disorders such as rheumatoid arthritis. Possibly, in a similar way, anxiety disorders represent an overactive anxiety system. Such an approach may be on the right lines but as it stands is too vague to be of much use or capable of testing. As with physical disease, mental disorders probably have a wide range of causes.

So far the evolutionary approach has generated a number of plausible hypotheses for mental abnormalities. They are reviewed in the next section.

Mental abnormalities: some hypotheses

Malfunctioning mental modules

If we take the modular view of the mind advocated by many evolutionary psychologists then it is possible to see some disorders as due to malfunctioning or even absent mental modules. One of the best-known cases of a disorder attributed to modular breakdown is autism. Baron-Cohen et al. (1985) and others have suggested that autism is best understood as a breakdown of a module or modules involved in the capacity called 'theory of mind'. This concept is discussed further in Chapter 8, but for present purposes we can understand theory of mind as the ability to attribute mental states to other humans and appreciate that other people have their own desires and beliefs which influence their behaviour. Autism is not a general impairment of cognition and there are some people with a variant of it called Asperger's syndrome who have high or normal IQs. One autistic individual with other talents was made the subject of a popular film called *The Rain Man*. The theory here is that autistic people find social life so difficult because they have no understanding of the behaviour of others. They often become withdrawn and uncommunicative. Other disorders for which this approach offers promising insights include Blair's account of psychopathy (a faulty violence inhibition module) and dysthymia (a faulty module dealing with reciprocal altruism). The interested reader is referred to a fuller discussion in Murphy and Stich (2000).

Exiles from Eden

Consider the following remark:

> I attribute the social and psychological problems of modern society to the fact that society requires people to live under conditions radically different from those under which the human race evolved.

These words were written by Theodore Kazcynski in his manifesto against the problems of urban civilisation. Whether Kazcynski is right or not he certainly had his own problems. He was the notorious 'unabomber' whom the US authorities spent 18 years trying to capture. Kazcynski killed three people and injured 21 more by sending parcel bombs. His manifesto against the evils of modern science and technology was printed in the *New York Times* when he threatened to kill again if they did not publish his views. He was finally caught in 1996 and is now serving four consecutive life sentences. Madman or prophet? Kazcynski may be something of both since several leading evolutionary psychologists do think that our genome may be out of step with our mode of existence.

Over the last 10,000 years, roughly since the invention of agriculture, humans have transformed their way of life so that for the majority of the world's 6 billion people conditions are now vastly different to the EEA. Could this transformation be the cause of many of today's psychiatric problems? Perhaps humans have trapped themselves in an air-conditioned zoo, showing many of the symptoms of caged animals. This view, sometimes called the 'genome lag' or 'exile from Eden' hypothesis, has attracted numerous adherents. Freud explored this general idea in his *Civilisation and its Discontents* (1930) and Jung in his *Modern Man in Search of Soul* (1933). The notion has a superficial plausibility: by abandoning the hunter-gatherer lifestyle to which we are genetically suited and moving to live in cities where some – the powerful few – accumulate fantastic power and wealth, we have set our genes and culture on a collision course. We have Stone Age genes and minds forced to live in a Space Age culture.

One area that may illustrate this approach is mate choice and estimations of self-worth. In choosing a mate an individual takes into account a number of factors but two essential ones are the attractiveness (fitness) of a potential spouse, judged by among other things physical signs of fecundity, health, resistance to disease and so on, coupled with some estimation of one's own sexual appeal. In pairing up, humans estimate their own relative attractiveness and circumstances before deciding what minimum level of attractiveness will suffice in a partner. Now in ancestral environments, where humans ranged in groups of about 100–150, such assessments were probably reasonably accurate. There would, for example, be very few extremely attractive or extremely wealthy people. The problem with modern culture is that people are now frequently exposed to images of highly desirable men and women in the form of fashion models, actors and actresses. The overall effect may be to bias our perception of the true frequency of such people in our social group. Men may become dissatisfied with their partners, thinking they have settled for someone too low down on the attractiveness scale; women may underrate their own attractiveness and take drastic actions, such as cosmetic surgery or crash dieting, to improve their appearance (Buss, 1996). In short, our ability to beam images of beautiful people around the globe may lead many to experience low self-esteem. Here is an example, then, where psychic distress may be caused by clever technologies and our twenty-first-century mode of existence.

Evaluation of this approach

So are our Stone Age genes and twenty-first-century mode of life out of alignment in other ways? This approach may have some merit but more work needs to be done. The problem is that despite abandoning the EEA, humans are thriving as never before. Compare the global population of *Homo sapiens* at 6 billion with that of our nearest relative, the common chimp (*Pan troglodytes*), at a few hundred thousand. Moreover, some psychiatric disorders, such as schizophrenia, seem to be present in all societies and are even found among the few genuine hunter-gatherer cultures left. The significance of this is that if schizophrenia is found in all cultures and even hunter-gatherers then since we evolved as hunter-gatherers we can hardly say that schizophrenia is solely a problem of living in a strange (to our genes) modern culture.

In an important article, Crawford (1998) suggests that we should look for similarities between ancient and current environments rather than differences. It is easy to draw sharp contrasts between ancestral and modern environments by choosing features that have drastically changed, such as population densities, jet travel, computers and so on. However, such a comparison is pointless unless we specify the nature of the adaptations that are supposed to be out of place as a result. We may live surrounded by Space Age technology but the fundamental patterns of life go on: couples meet and have babies; people make friends and enemies, argue and make up; we gossip intensely about each other and so on. Indeed, one of the ironies of the modern condition is that we launch high-tech satellites into orbit around the planet to beam down soap operas and pornography. Despite the dire prognostications of some science fiction writers that humans will become slaves to machines, looking at much modern technology and its uses it is clear that the contrary is more often the case: we have shaped our technology around our natures. Computers would much prefer to operate using instructions given in zeros and ones, yet we force them to communicate with us using little pictures and a clumsy mouse to point at them. 'The fundamental things apply as time goes by' so the old song goes.

There are other features of modern culture built around ourselves. We visit or live near to our relatives, houses are designed for the nuclear family, we work in groups with hierarchies – all these features are probably not far removed from the ancestral condition. Crawford advises that we should assume a basic similarity between ancient and contemporary environments with respect to particular adaptations unless there are signs of stress and malfunction in humans, or the behaviour is rare in the majority of cultures, or unusual reproductive consequences are observed. Polyandry (the sharing of one wife by several men), for example, is rare in human society and there are strong reasons for suspecting we are not adapted to this way of life.

No organism is perfect

Another problem with this whole area of research is that although *Homo sapiens* as a species evolved over the last 2 million years, and radically departed from a hunter-gatherer lifestyle about 10,000 years ago, we carry genes that were 'designed' long before that. Many of the genes for specific proteins we share with yeast, sea urchins, mice and even marigolds. So how far do we go back? It is possible, for example, to trace many of the physical problems that contemporary humans experience to periods long before the beginning of the Neolithic revolution. The agony and high risks of childbirth, although alleviated over the last 100 years by modern technology, are still serious problems for modern humans. The reason is that two evolutionary tendencies that almost define our humanity – bipedalism (walking upright) and a large brain – set off on a collision course some 2 million years ago. Our ancestors about 4 million years ago walked upright and this was possible with a bowl-shaped pelvis and a narrow birth canal. However, as our brains grew in size over the last 2 million years so it became increasingly difficult to squeeze a large head through a narrow opening. The solution natural selection gave us was premature birth. For a primate of our size, pregnancy should last about 21 months, but by that time the head of the infant would be too large to emerge – hence, our premature birth at 9 months followed by brain growth afterwards.

All this illustrates is that the whole of evolution is about compromises. The physical and psychological problems we now have may have deep-seated roots and not be just a product of abandoning some sort of the earthly paradise represented by the EEA. Put more generally, although natural selection has accomplished some amazing feats over the last three and a half billion years it has not produced perfect organisms.

The Neolithic revolution

If we are looking for an occasion when we most radically departed from the hunter-gatherer lifestyle which has characterised our social life for 90% of our time on this planet, then the first and perhaps the most important has to be the Neolithic revolution. During the Neolithic or 'New Stone Age' period humans moved from a position of foraging and hunting for food on a daily basis in small groups to a settled mode of existence involving the cultivation of crops and the domestication of animals, supplying food for thousands living together in cities. This revolution occurred about 10,000 years ago and current civilisation is based on it. If anything should have been a shock to our hunter-gatherer genes then this should be it. Beverly Strassmann and Robin Dunbar (1999) of the University of Liverpool have considered this point. Reviewing the evidence on the spread of farming and its replacement of hunter-gathering they note that the evidence suggests that agriculture supplanted hunter-gathering by a process of 'demic diffusion' rather than the spread of knowledge by traditional cultural means. This means that the agriculturists literally outbred the hunter-gatherers rather than passing on the good idea of agriculture by oral means and converting them from their way of life by persuasion. If they outbred them, it means that they were doing better in terms of reproductive success; all of which tends to throw doubt on the idea that agriculture represented a profound cultural and maladaptive shock.

However, life did become worse after the Neolithic revolution in a number of respects. The fact that agriculture could sustain a higher population density meant that the early farmers were much more subject to infectious disease. Population densities before this were so low that disease transmission would have been very slow. In addition, the increase in production of starch led to more dental problems – problems only exacerbated by the massive increase in consumption of refined sugars over the last 100 years.

This reminds us that those more recent features of our modern lifestyle rather than the move away from hunter-gathering itself may be responsible for some of our problems. Modern living conditions mean that traditional extended family networks become severely disrupted. If you have ever earned money by babysitting or have travelled more than 10 miles to visit a relative you are witnessing a phenomenon which would have appeared strange to our distant ancestor, who would probably have lived in close-knit groups with relatives helping with childbearing and childminding and visits to a relative being only a short walk away. This is not a trivial change since kin supply essential support for our physical and emotional well-being. Strassmann and Dunbar suggest that this loss of kin support may go a long way to explaining depressive illness.

Depression: a modern epidemic?

In Table 6.1 we show a ranking of what are known as disability-adjusted life years (DALYs) from a survey of 1996. The DALYs are calculated from loss of life due to the condition and years of life spent suffering with the condition adjusted for the severity of the condition. They provide a measure of the importance of various conditions to the global totals for human suffering.

The table serves to reinforce the point that childbirth is still an enormously risky activity. It is noteworthy, however, that depression ranks fourth in terms of a scale of global suffering. It would not be too far-fetched to say that based on this data the world is suffering from an epidemic of depression. In relation to this, Strassmann and Dunbar suggest that 'a contributing factor may be the breakdown of kin support networks and the attendant loss of psychological and material security' (Strassman and Dunbar, 1999, p. 100).

The conclusion of this section is that perhaps it is an over-generalisation to simply say that mental disorders are due to our genes not equipping us for life in the twenty-first century. We need to be more precise and specify exactly those features of modern life that may cause problems and how precisely they pose challenges to our biological and psychological needs.

Table 6.1 Leading causes of world DALYs, 1990		
Disease or injury	*1990 rank*	*Percentage of total DALYs*
Lower respiratory track infections (pneumonia)	1	8.2
Diarrhoea	2	7.2
Perinatal complications (low birthweight, birth trauma)	3	6.7
Unipolar major depression	4	3.7
Ischaemic heart disease	5	3.4
Data adapted from Murray and Lopez (1996).		

The adaptive conservatism hypothesis

The anxiety response and manifestations of overanxiousness can be seen in terms of an adaptive response to signals from the environment. Imagine one of our primate ancestors enjoying a nutritious meal of fruit from a forest tree when suddenly a rustling sound is heard. Should the primate ignore it and continue to feed or panic and flee? Making the right decision depends upon a number of factors, such as:

- The ratio of signal to noise. The noise could be that of a predator or simply a harmless animal or the sound of wind.
- The cost of mistakenly thinking the noise is that of a predator. In this case, the cost would be the loss of a useful source of nourishment.

- The cost of mistakenly ignoring the signal and continuing to feed even though it arose from a real predator. In this case, the cost could be death.

The balance of decision-making is a fine one and the advantage lies with the individual who has a finely tuned anxiety response. It is important to note, however, that the cost of death is much greater than the cost of missing a meal. Consequently, appearing more anxious than the occasion seems to demand could be adaptive. This is known as the adaptive conservatism hypothesis of fears. The problem with this approach is that it may be useful as a means of explaining why people are more anxious than they often need to be, but it falls short of being able to tackle why for some the anxiety is so great that they cease to function normally at all.

Preparedness theory

An important point to note is that fears and phobias are not randomly distributed. Very few people, for example, have phobias about pencil sharpeners but many more have phobias about small animals such as rats and spiders. Partly as a means of explaining this, in 1971 Seligman introduced his preparedness hypothesis. This states that the non-random distribution of fears is caused by an evolutionary predisposition (preparedness) that operates during fear conditioning. The important point here is that we are not born with innate fears, but we are born to more readily associate harm with some stimuli than others. More specifically, the hypothesis suggests that we become readily conditioned to fear objects that were once harmful to us in the EEA, but are more resistant to fears developing due to associations with harmless objects and events. Adverse experiences provide the trigger but adapted predispositions channel its effect. In a sense, this hypothesis is a mixture of adaptationist thinking with a Pavlovian conditioning interpretation.

This hypothesis makes at least two predictions that can be tested:

- Most phobias should relate to things that were harmful to early humans.
- Fear of these things will be easily acquired by test subjects since we are predisposed to associate adverse stimuli with them.

Lumsden and Wilson emphasised this point when they said:

> It is a remarkable fact that phobias are easily evoked by many of the greatest dangers of mankind's ancient environment, including closed spaces, heights, thunderstorms, running water, snakes and spiders. Of equal significance, phobias are rarely evoked by the greatest dangers of modern technological society, such as guns, knives, automobiles, and electric sockets. (Lumsden and Wilson, 1982, p. 2)

There is some evidence to show that these predictions are supported to a degree. Some of the most convincing studies come from work on illusory correlations. In these experiments, mild electric shocks are administered to volunteer subjects when images of objects are shown. In a study by Tomarken, Mineka and Cook, several objects were used including images of what were supposed to represent historically real risks such as snakes and spiders, and neutral images such as flowers or mushrooms. The linkage between the pain from the shock and the image was random but averaged 1/3 for each object. In other words, for every three images of the snake, flower or mushroom a painful shock was felt; the other two times either nothing was felt or an audible tone was heard. When the volunteers were asked afterwards to estimate the percentage of time a pain followed an image of a snake it was consistently overestimated at 42–52%, compared to the actual association of 33% (Tomarken, Mineka and Cook, 1989). Studies on other primates such as rhesus monkeys have also shown that monkeys can be made to acquire a persistent fear of snakes, whereas the same experimental design (showing video tapes of monkeys reacting fearfully to each stimuli to the test subjects) fails to produce a fear of flowers.

Against these positive findings must be balanced problems with the preparedness hypothesis. One methodological problem is that a priori knowledge of objects to which a subject is likely to be easily conditioned could affect the choice of stimuli by the experimenter. In other words, an experimenter might suspect that a phobia of snakes is more easily conditioned, choose this as a so-called ancestral hazard and then show that indeed such a fear is easily conditioned.

Perhaps a more serious problem concerns trying to identify what counts as an ancestral hazard (sometimes referred to in the literature as 'phylogenetically relevant stimuli'). Deciding on what were real risks to hominids half a million years ago necessarily involves a good deal of conjecture. We have to construct the past environment of these early humans and speculate on likely predators and sources of injury. Nor is this environment of evolutionary adaptation a single environment. We may spend a lot of time reconstructing the environment of the African savannah only to find that humans migrated out of Africa and then faced a whole new range of environments, including the snowy wastes of a Europe passing through various ice ages. The study of Tomarken, Mineka and Cook noted earlier can be revisited in the light of this difficulty. The positive interpretation of this experiment is that humans can be more readily conditioned to associate pain with images of snakes and spiders than flowers or mushrooms because the former were once hazardous to our ancestors and we are prepared to accept conditioning to them readily. But as Delprato pointed out:

> . . . considering the fact that approximately 100 species of poisonous mushrooms have been identified in the USA alone . . . , it is reasonable to suspect that mushrooms have posed a greater threat to the survival of the human species than have snakes and spiders combined. (Delprato, 1989, p. 89)

The other side of this critique is that some fears which we suppose to be ancestral may not have been that hazardous. Many people show a fear of spiders, but to what extent did spiders represent a significant threat to early humans? True, there are some poisonous spiders but these amount to only about 0.1% of the 35,000 documented species. It is hard to believe that these small creatures posed such a threat to our existence that we are now genetically programmed to become easily sensitised to painful associations with them.

There is also evidence that some phobias do arise in relation to objects and situations with little apparent relationship to past environments. Table 6.2 shows the results of a large survey on 20,000 subjects based on interviews and questionnaires administered in the USA. The second column shows the percentage of subjects expressing an 'unreasonable fear' and the third column the percentage that would meet the criterion of having a formal phobia diagnosis. Only the four more common phobias are shown. The results are interesting in that they show that unreasonable fears are widespread, with one in six people (18.5%) meeting the criteria for a formal phobia of something. The problem for the evolutionary paradigm is that whereas it is possible to weave a story explaining how bugs, snakes, mice and bats may have once been real hazards through direct attack or spreading disease, it is harder to relate public transport to the plains of the African savannah.

Table 6.2 Selection of results of an epidemiological study of phobias on a sample of 20,000 American subjects

Stimulus	% of subjects expressing unreasonable fear	% of subjects classifiable as having a phobia
Bugs, mice, snakes, bats	22.4	6.1
Heights	18.2	4.7
Water	12.5	3.3
Public transport	10.5	3.2
Any phobia	60.2	18.5

Data extracted from Chapman (1997, Table 20.3).

Other studies also show that phobias can develop in relation to recent (in evolutionary terms) scenarios. Kuch *et al.* (1994) report that 38% of survivors of road accidents develop a phobia related to driving a car. In another survey of common fears Kirkpatrick found the surprising result that of the 133 stimuli categories used, women rated fear of roller-coasters the most important. For men the fear of being punished by God was ranked the highest (Kirkpatrick, 1984). Evolutionary psychologists are an ingenious lot but even they would be hard pushed to give an adaptationist account of these findings.

As we saw in Table 5.1, phobias may represent extreme forms of perfectly natural and useful emotions. Possibly anxiety and a series of mild phobias represent the price we have to pay for ensuring that our genes stay clear of danger and survive long enough to replicate themselves. The fact that some people suffer more than others could then be explained by the normal distribution of these traits, as explored in the next section.

The normal distribution theory

Perhaps mental disorders are due to a combination of genes whose effects in some individuals place them at the extreme ends of a normal distribution of traits. If we take a parameter such as height then there are many genes that will determine how tall an individual will grow. Because of this, if we take a large sample then heights will be normally distributed about a mean value (although the mean will be different for men and women). Most people will lie a few inches either side of the mean, with relatively few adults above 6 feet 4 inches and few below 5 feet 1 inch. Possibly then those who suffer from disorders such as depression and excessive anxiety lie at the too sensitive end, whereas those who are reckless and high risk-takers lie at the other end (Figure 6.1). In this model people who are overanxious to the point that they seem abnormal were dealt a rather unlucky combination of genes at conception that put them at the extreme end of the normal response curve. Extremes are not unknown for a wide range of characteristics. Some people are extremely tall, for example, and this is not always a healthy condition.

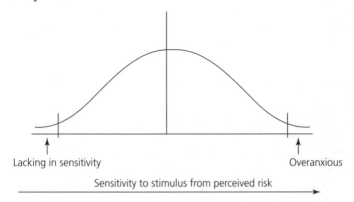

Lacking in sensitivity

Overanxious

Sensitivity to stimulus from perceived risk

Figure 6.1 A hypothetical normal distribution of the anxiety response

The problem with this approach is that although some authors, such as Stevens and Price (1996), consider it worthy of the title of a theory, it really is just a descriptive account of how some genes may be distributed. It is difficult to test if overanxious people simply have a good dose of anxiety-inducing genes.

Social homeostasis or rank theories of depression

Human social groups, including those currently living in EEA-like conditions, are hierarchical with constant tensions arising from the jockeying, especially among males, for rank and authority. In such groups, there are tensions and conflict arising constantly. It has been proposed that a condition such as depression serves to preserve the stability of the group. The argument is that by inducing lethargy and withdrawal in an individual who is likely to lose in a social contest, depression performs the valuable function of preventing further damaging conflict (Allen, 1995). In effect, depression is an act of sub-mission. Depression may not be a disorder per se but ideas like these suggest that what may seem counter-functional and bad for the organism may be effective in serving the longer-term interest of the individual who is suffering. This is sometimes called the rank theory of depression. The theory is difficult to test and it seems unlikely that it could be pressed much further to explain severe depression. Allen suggested that the depressive reaction had been selected by evolution 'whereas the clinically depressed state is a pathological aberration based on this adaptive emotional mechanism' (Allen, 1995). The problem here is that this merely shifts the burden of the explanation to the origins of the pathological aberration.

Ontogenetic or developmental theories

Using the analogy of the distribution of height again, we should note that height is a product of many genes but also many environmental influences; even identical (monozygotic) twins will grow to different heights if fed differently. Despite the appeal of the Swiss army knife model of mental modules of archetypes discussed earlier, it would obviously be wrong to suppose that the mind arrives on the world stage fully formed. What is more likely is that the brain is born with mental hardware and neural circuitry pre-formed to respond to stimuli in specific ways. Different environments will produce different people and adverse environments may produce distorted and poorly functioning archetypes or mental dispositions. The biologist Ernst Mayr used the term 'open programs' to describe how environmental conditions shape the tendencies in the genotypes to produce the phenotype.

You may now be thinking that this approach belongs to social psychology or developmental psychology, and you would be right. The reason it is included here is that evolution suggests the origin of the developmental programme that unfolds in relation to external stimuli as we mature. For example, humans are almost certainly programmed to bond affectionately with their mother. If this process is interrupted then abnormal psychological growth may result. In this sense, then, evolutionary theory provides the ultimate cause framework whereas psychoanalytical, behavioural and psychosocial models provide the proximate hypotheses (McGuire, Troisi and Raleigh, 1997).

A good example of an ontogenetic theory would be the ideas on attachment developed by the British doctor and psychoanalyst John Bowlby (1969). Bowlby proposed that all primates are born pre-programmed to form close emotional ties with nearby adults such as mothers. Bowlby argued that how a child conceived of social relationships later in life depended on this early infant experience and disruptions to this crucial early process of attachment could bring about disorders later in life.

In the 1930s, Bowlby worked as a psychiatrist at a centre for troubled youngsters in London. Here he was struck by the blank emotional response of many of the youths he met. Then he noticed a pattern: children who showed a lack of emotional response, and typically were in trouble with the authorities, tended to be those who had been separated from their mothers at an early age.

At the time of Bowlby's original insights, the study of human emotions and relationships was dominated by Freudian psychoanalysis. The study of non-human animals, particularly in America, was also heavily influenced by the behaviourism of Watson, Skinner and their followers. Bowlby felt that both Freudianism and behaviourism were not adequate to the task of explaining his observations on attachment. Fortuitously, Bowlby then came across the work of two men: the Cambridge comparative psychologist Robert Hinde and the Austrian ethologist Konrad Lorenz. Both were sensitive to the importance of evolutionary theory in explaining animal behaviour. This was just the encouragement that Bowlby needed and he went on to formulate his attachment theory within an evolutionary framework.

Bowlby suggested that the process of forming an attachment was adaptive for both parents and offspring. Babies, he argued, are born programmed to attach to the adult that gives them care early in life; this of course is usually the parent. This provides babies with a source of protection and nurture. From the point of view of the parent, the attachment process is essential to ensure that the parent looks after the carrier of its genetic investment. Genes that instruct a parent to take great care with its offspring will tend to thrive and spread since they will be found in that offspring. Bowlby argues that just as the newborn baby is attracted to the smiles and face of its mother, so the faces of babies and their voices serve to stimulate and release the nurturing response of the mother.

According to Bowlby, the attachment bond had to form before the age of 2½ years or else it would be difficult for an attachment to form after this. Should attachment not take place then permanent emotional damage would result.

Bowlby's work has had an enormous impact on thinking about the relationship between parents and children in the first few years of life. His work has been criticised, other possible explanations for the effects he observed have been offered, and others have extended and modified his ideas. However, the central tenets of attachment theory have entered mainstream psychological thinking and the consensus seems to be that attachment has an important role to play in the long-term mental health of the growing child. Where the theory is weak is in explaining why children differ so much in their resilience to neglect.

Here is not the place to thoroughly assess attachment theory and a good review can be found in another book in this series called *Early Socialisation: Sociability and attachment* by Cara Flanagan. The point of including it here is that it is an example of an evolutionary informed approach to mental health and an instructive example of how genes and environment interact in their effects on the growing organism.

Inclusive fitness theories

Inclusive fitness is a term that came into use after groundbreaking work by the theoretical biologist William Hamilton in 1964. For Darwin, fitness was a property of an organism (which included physical and behavioural features) that helped itself and its offspring survive. Hence, a mother will behave kindly towards her children at great expense to herself because children represent her genetic investment. One thing a human mother is assured of is that 50% of her genes are to be found in any of her children. This is not to suggest that the mother consciously calculates or reasons like this; evolution provided us with this response. What Hamilton realised was that copies of our genes are also to be found in other relatives. It would follow that individuals should also be kind to brothers, sisters and cousins since they too will contains copies of some of our genes. The chance of any one gene picked at random being found in another individual is called the **coefficient of genetic relatedness** ('r'). The r-value between you and a brother or sister by the same parent is 0.5; between yourself and a cousin 0.125; between yourself and an identical twin 1.0. The importance of inclusive fitness was first glimpsed by the English biologist Haldane in the 1930s when he amusingly told his friends while drinking in a London pub (somewhere along Euston Road) that he would lay down his life for at least an identical twin or eight cousins.

Insights from inclusive fitness have been used to tackle a number of human behavioural patterns. One of them is suicide. Before applying this idea to humans imagine yourself approaching a hive of bees and foolishly sticking in your hand to extract the honey, or worse still threaten the life of the queen. Very soon, you will be stung repeatedly. On examining your wounds, you will notice that at the site of each sting half the bee's abdomen is left in your skin. It is said of humans that 'greater love hath no man than he should lay down his life for his friend', yet in this respect we are matched by the humble honey bee (*Apis mellifera*); for the bees that have stung you will die – they have sacrificed themselves, apparently, to save the hive. This at any rate was the conventional explanation until inclusive fitness was understood. There are sound reasons for supposing that the bees are not saving the hive but simply saving their own genes; those that die by these suicidal actions in deterring an intruder such as yourself ensure that copies of their genes (and crucially the suicidal genes) carry on into the next generation by those left in the hive – in particular by the queen, to whom they are all related by an r-value of 0.5.

Moving now to humans, the evolutionary psychologist Denys de Catanzaro has suggested that humans commit suicide when they are no longer able to contribute to their own inclusive fitness. If an individual ever reaches the sorry state when he or she is acting as a burden to nearby kin, and actively reducing inclusive fitness by remaining alive and diverting resources from the family group, then there is a terrible logic favouring suicide. It makes genetic sense to end one's own life and allow your genes to prosper in others.

By conducting a survey on a variety of people, Cantazaro looked at correlations between 'suicidal ideation' (a measure of the intent of people in the sample to ever commit suicide) and events in their own life. He found that suicidal intent was positively correlated with the perceived burden on the individual's family and negatively correlated with measures of sexual success such as number of children or frequency of sexual activity (de Cantazaro, 1995). In other words, when individuals are performing badly in the heterosexual market, or are a drain on the resources of kin, they are more likely to entertain suicidal thoughts.

More work remains to be done in this area but it is likely that at best inclusive fitness provides only a partial explanation of suicide. Suicide also correlates with other social variables that are harder to explain by evolutionary reasoning.

A genetic basis for mental disorders

Evolutionary explanations of mental disorders have to confront the fact that some disorders seem to run in families and, although environmental influences in specific families play a role, the evidence also points towards a genetic basis. A genetic basis for mental disorders raises two sets of issues:

1. Do some people possess harmful genes that impede normal human development and functioning?
2. Why do such genes exist if natural selection operates to remove the unfit and preserve the fit?

We should not be surprised if the answer to the first question is 'yes' since many physical disorders (e.g. Huntingdon's disease, cystic fibrosis, phenylketonuria, sickle cell anaemia and achondroplasia) can be shown conclusively to have a genetic basis. The fact that this is the case then poses a special question for the notion that our genes have become adpated to life through natural selection. This latter problem is tackled in the section on 'The adaptive value of genetically based disorders' below.

Unipolar and bipolar depression

The term unipolar refers to the fact that in people who suffer from this condition there is one abnormal state: that of depression with all its associated symptoms. It is sometimes thought that there are two discrete categories of unipolar depression: reactive and endogenous. Reactive depression is a response to some painful event such as loss of a loved one, redundancy at work or an instance of personal failure. Endogenous depression arises from inside the person and is usually more serious. These terms are not used in the DSM but instead we find major depressive disorder (MDD), which is severe but short lived, and dysthymic disorder, which is less acute but may last for much longer.

As the term bipolar indicates, in this condition there are two states, often called mania and depression. People afflicted by this condition (many of whom in history have been talented and creative people) experience violent mood swings, from mania, with its typical frantic activity, irritability, recklessness and increase in sexual energy, to depression itself.

There is evidence of some genetic basis to bipolar depression but little for unipolar depression. Studies on twins by Price (1968) found that monozygotic twins were much more likely to both suffer from manic depression if either one of them did than were non-identical or dizygotic twins. Significantly, this was observed even if the mono-zygotic twins were reared apart. Studies on children adopted by healthy couples have also shown that an individual is far more predisposed to manic depression if their biological parents also suffered from the disorder.

Schizophrenia

Schizophrenia is a complex condition involving disturbances to cognition, emotions and behaviour. The range of these symptoms is such that various attempts have been made to classify schizophrenia into a number of types. The DSM lists three: paranoid, involving hallucinations and delusions; disorganised, involving poorly coordinated speech and disorganised behaviour; and catatonic, involving apathy and lack of drive. Schizophrenia usually strikes men in their late teens or early twenties and women in their late twenties. It can blight what seem to be promising careers and although drugs can ameliorate the symptoms there is no known cure. The prevalence in populations has been estimated from different studies to be between 0.2% and 2.0%; this is often approximated to an incidence of 1% across all populations.

Like bipolar depression, there seems to be a genetic component. Table 6.3 uses the concept of r-value discussed earlier to tabulate the probability of developing schizophrenia if the other relative has the condition.

Table 6.3 Probability of developing schizophrenia (note that the average probability for any person is 0.01)

Relationship	r-value	Probability of developing schizophrenia if relative has the condition
MZ twins	1	0.48
DZ twins	0.5	0.17
Siblings	0.5	0.09
Grandchildren of a grandparent	0.25	0.05

We should note that no studies have shown concordance levels of 100%. This indicates that although there may be a genetic component to schizophrenia, environmental influences are also at work. Both the onset of schizophrenia and the course that it takes may be strongly influenced by the social dynamics of family life.

Another useful concept that assists the study of the heritability of psychiatric disorders is that of relative risk (lambda$_R$) which is defined as:

$$\text{Lambda}_R = \frac{\text{Risk or incidence of disorder among relatives of those affected}}{\text{Risk or incidence in general population}}$$

When the relatives in question are siblings (brothers or sisters), then the term becomes lambda$_S$. So lambda$_S$ becomes:

$$\text{Lambda}_S = \frac{\text{Risk to an individual if his/her brother or sister is affected}}{\text{Risk or incidence in general population}}$$

Table 6.4 shows some lambda$_S$ values for a variety of disorders. Diabetes, although obviously not a mental disorder, is included to illustrate the fact that such studies can help to establish if the condition has a heritable component. In this case, we note that diabetes type I is more strongly inherited than type II. If we compare Table 6.3 with Table 6.4 we can express the genetic basis of, say, schizophrenia in words. If your brother or sister has schizophrenia, you are 10 times more likely to develop the condition than the average member of the population (Table 6.4). In this case, your overall probability of developing the disease is 0.09 or about 1 in 10 (Table 6.3). If a probability of 1 in 10 is 10 times the average incidence then the average incidence among the general population is about 1 in 100.

We should treat these statistics with caution. The fact that you are 10 times more likely than average to develop schizophrenia if you have a brother or sister with the condition does not mean that there is a one-to-one correspondence between genes and the disease. It could be that you are more likely because you have been exposed to similar conditions to a brother or sister. Another alternative is that you carry genes that dispose you to react in certain ways to environmental stimuli. Table 6.3 shows that you have a 48% chance of contracting the disease if you have an identical twin with the condition. This leaves a 52% chance of not developing schizophrenia, yet your genes in this monozygotic condition are identical to those of your brother or sister. This shows that the relationship between genetic inheritance and the disorder is not simple.

Table 6.4 Approximate risk ratios for various disorders	
Disorder	Approximate risk ratio (lambda$_s$)
Autism	>75
Type I diabetes	20
Schizophrenia	10
Bipolar disorder	10
Panic disorder	5–10
Type II diabetes	3.5
Phobic disorders	3
Major depressive disorder	2–3
Data from Smoller and Tsuang (1998).	

The risks of mental disorders

Using Tables 6.3 and 6.4, and the above text, answer the following questions:

1. What is the average probability that an individual will develop schizophrenia if
   (a) there is no evidence of the condition in the family?
   (b) the grandparent of the individual is a sufferer?
2. If the risk of a bipolar disorder in the general population is 1.5%, what is the risk an individual will develop this condition if their brother already shows signs of the disease?

Depression and mania

People who suffer from a bipolar depressive disorder experience mood swings ranging from depression to mania, or its milder form hypomania. The table below shows how personality features can be described in terms of the depressed state or the mania state. Complete the table by correctly placing the terms at the bottom. The first two have already been completed for you.

Contrasting states of depression and mania in bipolar depressive disorders

Feature	Depressed state	Mania
Mood	Depressed	Elated
Self-esteem	Low	High
Appearance		
Social manner		
Speech		
View of future		
Sexual libido		

Terms: *drab and scruffy, submissive, rapid, optimistic, increased, pessimistic, domineering, smart and flamboyant, slow, reduced*

The adaptive value of genetically based disorders

If there is a genetic basis to such disorders as bipolar depression and schizophrenia, albeit only as a contributing factor, what are such genes doing remaining in the gene pool? We would expect that ill-suited genes would have been 'weeded out' by natural and sexual selection long ago. Moreover, the fact that the condition of schizophrenia, for example, is widely distributed in human populations suggests that it is not a recent arrival, awaiting eradication by the reduced fertility of schizophrenics, but that it has been part of the human condition for a very long time.

There are two types of standard response to this conundrum. The first is to suggest that the gene for the maladaptive trait in question is linked in some way to other genes that enhance fitness. This is sometimes called the **pleiotropy** hypothesis. Pleiotropy refers to the well-documented genetic fact that a gene or set of genes can have more than one effect. People prone to manic depression, for example, may also be highly creative. This could have helped our ancestors find solutions to tricky environmental problems that they encountered. The ability to find novel ways to obtain food, build shelters or escape predators would have been an extremely valuable asset during our evolution. The second type of response is to argue that the same genes that cause depression in some people give rise to effects in others that increase their fertility. This is an argument that has been applied to explain the possible genetic basis of male homosexuality. A gene for male homosexuality could thrive in the gene pool if, when found in the sisters of homosexuals, it increases their fertility.

There are a number of well-established cases of maladaptive genes surviving against apparent odds in the human gene pool. A simple change to the base sequence on our DNA is known to cause the distressing condition of sickle-cell anaemia. The substitution of one amino acid (glutamine becomes valine) in haemoglobin causes an alteration in the shape of red blood cells – they appear sickle shaped – and a reduction in the oxygen-carrying capacity of the blood. The sickle-shaped cells produced when the defective gene is present on both **chromosomes** (i.e. the chromosomes are homozygous) are quickly broken down by the body; blood does not flow smoothly and parts of the body are deprived of oxygen. The physical symptoms range from anaemia, physical weakness, damage to major organs, brain damage and heart failure. There is no cure for the condition, which causes the death of about 100,000 people worldwide each year. Sickle-cell anaemia is by far the most common inherited disorder among African-Americans and affects 1 in 500 of all African-American children born in the USA. Its high frequency in the population, and the fact that natural selection has not eliminated it (many of those suffering die before they can reproduce), is probably due to the fact that in Africa possession of one copy of the sickle-cell gene confers some resistance to malaria. If Hb is taken to be the normal haemoglobin gene and Hbs the sickle cell gene then people who inherit both sickle-cell genes, i.e. one from their father and one from their mother, and who are therefore

Hbs Hbs, suffer from sickle-cell anaemia and die young. People who inherit only one copy of the sickle-cell gene and are Hb Hbs are said to have sickle-cell trait and only some of the red blood cells are oddly shaped. It is in this latter condition that the gene gives an advantage in protecting against malaria since the malarial parasite (*Plasmodium*) cannot complete its life cycle in the mutant cells. It is the prevalence of malaria in African countries that explains why this apparently maladaptive gene survived in the gene pool and is now found among African-Americans.

Just how small an advantage is needed to ensure that genes that are maladaptive when an individual carrier copies from both parents can also be seen in the condition of cystic fibrosis. A child with cystic fibrosis is born when the relevant genes are homozygous in the recessive state; that is, it has two copies of the defective gene: one from each parent. If it has only one copy then it is said to be a carrier. People who are carriers live perfectly normal and healthy lives, never realising they are carriers until they mate with another carrier. About 1 in 25 Caucasians are thought to be 'carriers' of the recessive allele for cystic fibrosis. The chance of two carriers meeting is thus about $(\frac{1}{25})^2 = 1$ in 625 or 0.0016. The chance of a child from a union of these parents having both recessive alleles and hence displaying the condition is one quarter of 0.0016 = 0.0004, or 1 in 2500. Hence about 1 in 2500 of Caucasian children are born with cystic fibrosis (see 'Case study: the avoidance of incest' in Chapter 1). Simply removing those affected by cystic fibrosis, i.e. those who are homozygous, will not remove the allele itself. In fact the heterozygous condition only needs to carry a 2.3% advantage compared to non-carriers for the recessive allele to persist indefinitely (see Strachan and Read, 1996).

Schizophrenia: the group-splitting hypothesis

Stevens and Price (1996) have proposed a novel hypothesis for the persistence of schizophrenia. They suggest that schizoid personalities could have acted in the past to perform the valuable function of dividing human groups when they become too large.

Humans are, without doubt, social primates. Our inherited biological capacity for complex language, shared by no other animal, shows that group living has been a fundamental component of human evolution. Scientists differ over dating the origin of human language, but if we take 100,000 years ago as a conservative estimate then it is hard to imagine what humans used language for if not to facilitate group living. We may say that language indicates group living although group living does not always lead to language. As an illustration of this, our nearest relatives, the chimps, also live in large stable groups but without the capacity for language. Our very psychology seems geared up for group dynamics. When strangers assemble they readily form groups; our moral behaviour all too readily seems to distinguish between the in-group and the out-group – a disposition all too easily exploited for tribal conflict and warfare.

Group living carries benefits and drawbacks and all groups have their optimum size. As the size of a group increases so more eyes and brains become available to watch out for predators and to find food. However, beyond a certain size, characteristic of the species and the environment in which it lives, negative effects begin to outweigh the advantages. Food may be more easily spotted but then there are more mouths to feed and the share for each is reduced. This means that the group travel over a greater home range to find food of sufficient quantity, but as the travel distance increases so does the energy used in finding food and so do the risks from predators. It follows that as a group grows in size through reproduction, or the influx of outsiders, there comes a point when the optimum group size is exceeded and fission will increase the fitness of each individual. Stevens and Price estimate that the critical size of early hunter-gatherer groups may have been 40–60. Dunbar, also keenly aware of the importance of group dynamics in the evolution of humans, puts this figure somewhere between 100 and 150 (Dunbar, 1996). Whatever the group size when fission occurs, the argument is that groups would be persuaded to split by a charismatic leader who would promise benefits from those who would follow him (or her). Stevens and Price maintain that it is the symptoms of a schizoid personality, such as cognitive dissonance, mood changes, bizarre beliefs, hallucinations and delusions of grandeur, that would have induced others, already discontented by the conditions prevailing in a group beginning to exceed its optimum size, to follow and form a new community.

The problem with this hypothesis is that it is very difficult to test. It could be possible to examine if cult leaders show signs of a schizoid personality but extremely difficult to show that such personality types formed a significant part of our evolutionary history. Stevens and Price are aware that suggestions that changes in gene frequencies can favour groups are unpopular now in evolutionary biology. The prevailing paradigm, with a few exceptions, is that evolution only benefits the individual and that characteristics that favour groups are unlikely to evolve since competition between groups is too slow compared to competition between individuals. The debate here is a complex one and will be resolved within the discipline of evolutionary biology itself so you should not worry about it here.

Evolutionary psychiatry: prospects

The evolutionary approach to mental disorders is still at an embryonic stage, or at best in its infancy. Against this immaturity, however, we should also remember that contemporary mainstream psychiatry is still nowhere near the stage of established medicine as a discipline or series of approaches based on a coherent body of evidence and theory. Nesse and Williams criticise most current psychiatry for putting the cart before the horse, for 'trying to find the flaws that cause the disease without understanding normal functions of the mechanisms' (Nesse and Williams, 1995, p. 230). As an analogy they consider coughing. The traditional psychiatric approach, parodied by these authors, would be to describe and catalogue coughing, study the neural mechanisms at work when coughing takes place and identify the cough control centre in the brain. Psychiatrists would then proceed to observe how certain substances, like codeine, suppress coughing, leading to speculations that coughing may be the result of a lack of natural codeine-like substances in the body. Amidst all this, how much clearer it becomes when we know that coughing is a natural defensive reaction of the body to expel foreign matter from the lungs, the oesophagus or the mouth. The analogy is of course an oversimplification. However, it is a powerful one when taken as a more general statement that the best way to progress in understanding the mind is to establish the purposes for which it was designed. In this respect evolutionary psychology, even if it never fulfils its claim to provide a unifying base for the whole of psychology, will have much to offer. An approach based on an understanding of the design of the human mind would also help enormously in the classification of mental disorders and overcome some of the objections discussed earlier to the DSM system. If we properly understood the adaptive purposes of the various components or modules of the human mind we would be able to distinguish those disorders such as autism, where the module is not functioning, from others where the module is functioning as it was intended to but where the environment now is vastly different from the environment in which it evolved to perform its task. These might be called the 'out of Eden disorders' discussed in an earlier section. If this approach is successful we may also have to face the chilling prospect that some conditions that we classify as disorders are perfectly adaptive from an individual point of view and their mental modules are functioning just as nature intended. Antisocial personality disorders, for example, may be quite effective at allowing an individual to satisfy his or her desires and reproductive interests even though it causes suffering for others. In a similar speculative vein, the fact that someone lacks or has a reduced sense of guilt or remorse might be quite adaptive for an individual but cause problems for their social group.

Currently though, evolutionary psychologists have to face up to the fact that compared to their successes in explaining human sexual behaviour accounts of mental disorders have met with only limited experimental support. Moreover, the hypotheses proposed are often difficult to test. This does not mean they are wrong – correct explanations may be difficult to test directly – but until more experimental and quantitative support is forthcoming the criticism that evolutionary accounts of mental disorders resemble a series of fanciful stories will be difficult to shake off.

The human mind is a complex entity, and compared to the spectacular successes of the sciences of chemistry, physics and biology in the realm of the organic and physical world, psychology has only just begun to penetrate the labyrinths of its own subject matter. This complexity comes about because the human mind is a product of a large brain. Exactly why the human brain grew so large, and the relationship between brain size and intelligence, are the subjects of the next chapter.

Summary

• A number of ultimate or functional explanations have been advanced to account for the existence of mental disorders. These are:

    (i) That disorders result when mental modules designed through evolution for specific tasks malfunction or are defective at birth.

(ii) That disorders result from the fact that our genomes are maladapted to the modern world ('exiles of Eden hypothesis').

(iii) That overanxiety and excessive sensitivity are sensible adaptations to ensure that we avoid unnecessary risks ('adaptive conservatism hypothesis').

(iv) That the mind has been pre-prepared through evolution to become easily conditioned to stimuli that were once harmful. Hence people readily develop phobias in relation to snakes but *r* in relation to electrical sockets, although the latter present a greater danger today for most people.

(v) That disorders are part of a spread of temperaments. Sufferers lie at an extreme end of a normal distribution ('normal distribution theory').

(vi) Depression among those who are not competing well serves to ensure the cohesion of the group ('social homeostasis theory' or 'rank theory of depression').

(vii) That extreme depression, followed by suicide, may be a subtle way of genes ensuring their own increased survival in relatives ('inclusive fitness theories').

- There is a good deal of evidence that bipolar depressive disorders and schizophrenia have a genetic basis. One way to explain the fact that such genes have not been eliminated by natural selection is to suggest that they also confer some advantage (in terms of reproductive fitness) on those that carry them.

The following accounts are very brief clinical case summaries of the suffering experienced by a number of different people. For each individual, relate their case to a particular condition or a particular theoretical perspective on the causes of mental disorders discussed in this chapter.

(a) John is a chemical engineer. In order to earn more money for his family he decided to works night-shifts in the control room of the plant. The plant does not close at night and produces its product continually. After about 4 weeks of night work John complained of depression, irritability and mood swings.

Review exercise

(b) Kevin is a fashion designer. His highly creative designs have won numerous rewards and financially he is very successful. However, he is now in his fourth marriage. The pattern is that he has highly creative periods when he is happy, active and extremely energetic. During these periods, he is attractive to the opposite sex. Such periods are followed by long bouts of depression that often lead to a failure in his relationships.

(c) Martha was an elderly lady confined to a nursing home. She felt lonely there and her life seemed to have little meaning. Moreover, the home was costing her thousands each month. Sadly she took her life and left her considerable savings to her grandchildren.

(d) James is a lorry driver. He is 5 stone overweight and has a history of circulatory problems. Once he nearly fell from the top of a lorry but was saved by a friend. He now has a phobia about heights and finds it difficult to ascend tall buildings. His complaints about his poor circulation have met with advice from doctors, who tell him to cut down on fat in his diet and take more exercise. James tends to ignore this advice: he enjoys fatty food and can't accept that it is harming him. He worries more about his phobia of heights than his diet.

Further reading

There are very few books addressed to students below undergraduate level on the evolutionary approach to mental disorders, but the following texts may be accessible.

Baron-Cohen, S. (1997). *The Maladapted Mind*. Hove, UK: Psychology Press. See the Preface and Chapters 1, 4 and 12.

Merckelbach, H. and Jong, P.J. (1997). Evolutionary models of phobias. In G.L. Davey (ed.) *Phobias. A handbook of Theory, Research and Treatment*. Chichester, UK: Wiley. A useful chapter that gives a cautious and critical review of the evolutionary approach.

Nesse, R.M. and Williams, G.C. (1995). *Evolution and Healing*. London: Weidenfeld & Nicolson. A readable survey of the whole topic of what is sometimes called Darwinian medicine. Chapters 1, 2 and 14 are the most useful for this chapter.

Stearns, S.C. (ed.) (1999). *Evolution in Health and Disease*. Oxford: Oxford University Press. A book based on a high-level conference held in Switzerland in 1997. It reports on some interesting research findings. The most suitable chapters for this section are 1, 8 and 23.

Stevens, A. and Price, J. (1996). *Evolutionary Psychiatry*. London: Routledge. One of the few books dealing solely with this topic. It should be accessible to the good A-level candidate. See Chapters 1, 2, 3, 5, 8 and 13.

7

The evolution of brain size

◈ The place of humans in nature
◈ The importance of size
◈ Brain size and the risks of childbirth
◈ Brain size and scaling effects (allometry): a mathematical
  diversion
◈ Ancestral brains
◈ Summary

The place of humans in nature

In the *Origin of Species* (1859) Darwin was decidedly coy about the
application of his ideas to humans. This was probably a wise strategy
and ensured that he avoided at least some of the vitriolic commentary
that had befallen earlier attempts to discuss the evolution of mankind.
The implications in Darwin's book were clear enough, but the fatal
body blows to those that still clung to the view of humans as occupying
a special place in creation were delivered by Huxley in 1863 in his
Man's Place in Nature and then later by Darwin himself in *The Descent
of Man* (1871). Darwin's belief that humans were descended from a
common ancestor with the African apes has since been confirmed as
substantially correct. The modern classification of animals in the taxa
appropriate to humans is shown in Figure 7.1.

Do not be too put off by the Latin names that biologists use for
their schemes of classification (taxonomy). It is really just a hierarchical

Kingdom: Animalia

Phylum: Chordata

Class: Mammalia

Order: Primates

Infraorder: Anthropoidea

Superfamily: Hominoidea

Family: Hominidae

Genus: *Homo*

Species: *Homo sapiens*

Figure 7.1 **Traditional taxonomy of the human species**

way of classifying organisms by their relationship to each other. It is possible to do the same sort of thing with motor cars. Imagine that you own a Peugeot 206, 3-door saloon, XL. It could be classified as follows:

Kingdom: Machines

Phylum: Self-propelled

Class: Petrol-engined

Order: Motor vehicle

Family: Saloon cars

Genus: Peugeot

Species: 206, 3-door XL

The great advantage of the biological system is that properly done it enables evolutionary relationships to be examined. According to modern classification, we share our place in the family Hominidae with chimps and gorillas. This would mean that the term hominids should strictly be taken to include humans, chimps and gorillas. The convention remains, however – a relic from a previous system – that the term **hominid** only refers to modern humans and their ancestors. We will keep to this convention here. But note that humans belong to the order of primates and so when in this chapter we use the term primate this must be taken to include humans as well.

What is indisputable is that humans (*Homo sapiens*) are now the only species left in the genus *Homo*. But there were once other species such as *Homo habilis* and *Homo erectus*. Figure 7.2 shows a time chart of early hominids.

The importance of size

Our remote ancestors among the **Australopithecines** were small and adults probably stood no more than about 4 feet high, but as the hominid line evolved so body size grew. One effect of the increase in body size was that the absolute requirement for calorie intake also grew – larger bodies need more food to fuel them. The consequence for hominids of the larger amount of food that had to be found was that their home range increased. This was not the only option available, of course. Gorillas, for example, grew in size but became adapted to eating large quantities of low-calorie foodstuffs, such as leaves. This requires a large body to contain enough gut to digest the plant material and this is essentially the strategy pursued by large herbivores such as cattle. Chimps and early humans clearly opted for the high-calorie mixed diet, however, that required clever foraging to obtain. Larger animals also take longer to mature sexually and so offspring become expensive to produce and require longer periods of care. The kin group and larger social groups now become important for care and protection (see Foley, 1987).

Increases in size may in themselves have been a response to ecological factors (e.g. climate change) but it is important to note that such increases can have profound effects on the lifestyle of an animal and, through complex feedback effects, force it to adapt further in other ways. Large animals, for example, have a smaller surface area-to-volume ratio than small ones and in tropical climates this would lead to problems of overheating and, consequently, a greater reliance on water. The upright stance of hominids may have been a response to this, since standing upright exposes less surface area to the warming rays of the sun. The loss of body fur would also have helped with temperature regulation. It is interesting that humans have just as many follicles as the great apes but the hairs emerging do not grow very long. Here we have a seeming paradox. Humans may have lost hair to keep cool but other tropical primates (gorillas, chimps, and orang-utans)

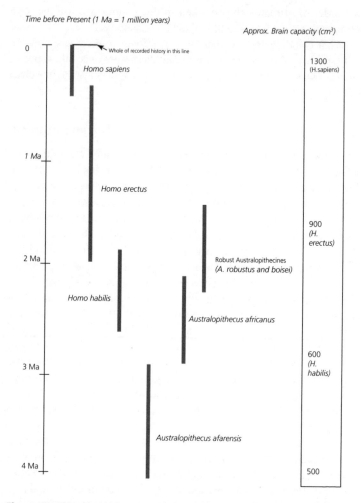

Time before Present (1 Ma = 1 million years)

Approx. Brain capacity (cm³)

0

Whole of recorded history in this line

Homo sapiens

1300
(H.sapiens)

1 Ma

Homo erectus

900
(H.
erectus)

2 Ma

Robust Australopithecines
(A. robustus and boisei)

Homo habilis

Australopithecus africanus

600
(H.
habilis)

3 Ma

Australopithecus afarensis

4 Ma

500

Figure 7.2 **Time chart of some early hominids. The exact lineages (i.e. which species descended from which) remain uncertain and controversial and so no linkages are shown here. Source of data: Holloway (1999)**

have retained theirs. In fact, the tropical animals that have lost their hair tend to be large mammals such as elephants and hippopotami that have thick heavy skin, quite unlike humans in every respect. Moreover, retaining body hair would have been useful to protect against the sun's rays and to help insulate the body as humans moved to northerly latitudes. It begins to look as if the glib explanation of humans having lost body hair to keep cool in hot climates is something of a convenient story rather than a testable scientific proposition. If we probe deeper, however, plausibility reasserts itself. Most tropical carnivores hunt at night, dawn or dusk when the temperature is cooler. In addition, the other primates, like most mammals, sweat very little. It is likely that early humans hunted during daylight hours and like us were prone to sweat following physical exertion. The scenario then is that humans lost their body hair to dissipate the heat generated from daytime physical activity in a hot climate. To assist this process they also evolved sweat glands. A fact of significance here, and consistent with this interpretation, is the observation that humans retained hair on the head. The reason for this is probably that although the brain uses a significant amount of energy while the body is at rest, the brain is not a muscle and so physical activity does not discharge a lot of waste heat into this region. Far better then to keep hair on the top of the head, which will help in protection from sunlight, and lose hair where heat is generated. This loss of hair was to be a problem for our ancestors as they moved out of Africa to northern Europe and faced a series of ice ages. But the loss of body hair occurred before this drift out of Africa and, fortunately for our survival, by this time our brains had grown to a size whereby we could fathom out how to survive using tools, clothing and fire.

The most remarkable feature of the period between the Australopithecines and *Homo sapiens*, however, is that brains grew larger than expected from body size increases alone (see section on 'Brain size and scaling effects' below). This is noteworthy because our brains are expensive to run. A chimp devotes 8% of its basal metabolic rate to maintaining a healthy brain whereas for humans the figure is 22%, even though the human brain represents only about 2% of body mass. In other words 22 out of every 100 calories you use while resting go to brain maintenance. Larger brains require better sources of nourishment. Significantly, the initial increase in brain size about 2 million years ago does seem to correlate with a switch from a largely vegetation-based diet of Australopithecines to a diet with a higher percentage of meat as found with *Homo habilis*. This association could imply that the mental demands of meat eating (hunting and processing of food) could have stimulated an increase in brain size; or alternatively, some other factor drove up brain size and forced hominids into meat eating as a way of supplying the larger brain with nourishment.

Brain size and the risks of childbirth

The causes of the rapid growth of the human brain remains one of the most disputed subjects in human evolution. Whatever the cause, an increase in brain size posed at least two problems for early hominids: how to obtain enough nourishment to support energetically expensive neural tissue, and how to give birth to human babies with large heads. The first of these problems, as noted above, was probably solved by a switch to a meat-eating diet about 2 million years ago. The second problem was solved by what is, in effect, a premature birth of all human babies. One way to squeeze a large-brained infant through a pelvic canal is to allow the brain to continue to grow after birth. In non-human primates the rate of brain growth slows relative to body growth after birth. Non-human primate mothers have a relatively easy time and birth is usually over in a few minutes. Human mothers suffer hours of childbirth pains and the brain of the infant still continues to grow at pre-birth rates for about another 13 months. Measured in terms of brain weight development, if we were like other primates a full term for a human pregnancy would be about 21 months, by which time the head of the infant would be too large to pass through the pelvic canal. As in so many other ways, natural selection has forced a compromise between the benefits of bipedalism (requiring a small pelvis for ease of locomotion) and the risks to mother and child during and after childbirth. Human infants are born, effectively, 12 months premature.

Brain size and mating behaviour

The premature birth of human infants required a different social system for its support than the uni-male groups of our distant Australopithecine ancestors. As brain size grew so infants became more dependent on parental care. Women would have used strategies to ensure that care was extracted from males. This would lead to a more monogamous mating pattern emerging since a single male could not provide the care needed for many females. It is significant that body size sexual dimorphism of hominids during the Australopithecine phase was such that males were sometimes 50% larger than females. This dimorphism was probably selected by intrasexual selection as males fought with males to control sizeable harems. By the time of *Homo sapiens* this had reduced to 10–20%, signalling a move away from polygyny towards monogamy. One possibility is that women ensured male care and provisioning for offspring by the evolution of concealed ovulation. The continual sexual receptivity of the female and the low probability of conception per act of intercourse may have ensured that males remained attentive. The question as to why human females evolved and lost outward signs of ovulation while other primates such as chimps retained them is a difficult question, however. Theories abound, but it looks increasingly likely that the concealment of ovulation was a master move by women in the evolutionary game of sexual politics (Diamond, 1997).

Brain size and scaling effects (allometry): a mathematical diversion

Since Darwin and others traced our ancestry from other primates in the nineteenth century, there have been numerous attempts to establish what aspects of the human brain give humans their unique qualities. It is tempting to think that we simply have bigger brains than other mammals, but even a cursory examination of the evidence rules this out. Elephants have brains four times the size of our own and there are species of whales with brains five times larger than the average human brain. We should expect this, of course – larger bodies need larger brains to operate them. The next step might be to compare the relative size of brains (i.e. brain mass/body mass) among mammals. The results are not edifying: we are now outclassed by such modest primates as the mouse lemur (*Microcebus murinus*) which has a relative brain size of 3% compared to 2% for humans.

We can find some insight, however, in the phenomenon of 'allometry': as an organism increases in size there is no reason to expect the dimensions of its parts, such as limbs or internal organs, to increase in proportion to mass or volume. If we simply magnified a mouse to the size of an elephant, its legs would still be thinner in proportion to its body than those of an elephant. Returning to the relationship between brain and body size there exists a formula for mammals that works quite well:

Brain size = $C \times$ (Body mass)^k (1)

where C and k are constants. The constant C represents the brain weight of a hypothetical adult animal weighing 1 g. The constant k indicates how the brain scales with increasing body size and seems to depend upon the taxonomic group in question. Much of the pioneering work in developing these equations was done by Jerison (1973), who concluded that for the entire class of mammals k was about 0.67 and C about 0.12. There is much discussion about the precise values for these constants and even within primate groups k varies from 0.66 to 0.88. Later revisions of Jerison's work suggest k may be 0.76 for primates and C about 0.099 (Holloway, 1999).

If we plot a graph of brain size against body weight for mammals on linear scales a curve results, showing that brain size grows more slowly than body size (Figure 7.3).

Formulae like the one in Figure 7.3 can be made to yield straight lines if logs of both sides of the equation are taken. The way such equations work is such that if

Brain size = 0.099 (Body) $^{0.76}$

then

log (Brain size) = log [0.099 (Body) $^{0.76}$]

this expands to give

log (Brain size) = 0.76 log (Body mass) + log 0.099

Note that all the weights for this formula must be expressed in grams. So a plot of the logs of brain and body size or a plot on logarithmic scales should give a straight line of slope 0.76 (Figure 7.4).

Do not be too put off by the mathematics here – the important point to grasp is that humans have brains larger than would be expected in a mammal of our size. Thus, Figure 7.4 starts to give an indication of what makes humans so special: we lie well above the allometric line linking body weight and brain weight for other primates. If we insert a value of 65 kg as a typical body mass for humans into Equation (1) our brains should weigh about 780 g. In fact, the real figure is about 1330 g. Our brains are about twice the size expected for a primate of our body mass.

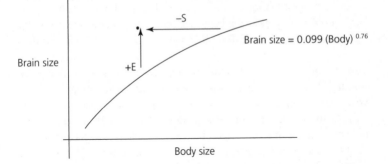

Figure 7.3 Growth of brain size in relation to body size for mammals. An animal occupying a point above the line is said to be encephalised, that is, it has a brain larger than expected for an animal of its body mass. This could be the result of a relative growth in brain size (positive encephalisation, +E) or a diminution of body size relative to brain mass (negative somatisation −S) (see Deacon, 1997)

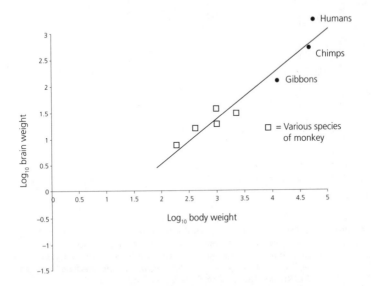

Figure 7.4 Logarithmic plot of brain size against body size. The line of best fit is drawn as log (brain size) = 0.76 log (body size) + log 0.099, hence brain size = 0.099 (body size)$^{0.76}$

Ancestral brains

A reasonable estimation of the size of the brains of our early ancestors can be obtained by taking endocasts of the cranial cavity in fossil skulls. This means filling the skull with some substance that fills it and then emptying it out and measuring its volume. There is some debate over how to interpret the fine detail of these casts (such as evidence for folding), but there is consensus on the general trend: about 2 million years ago the brains of hominids underwent a rapid expansion (Figure 7.5). Australopithecines possessed brains of a size to be expected from typical primates of their stature, but *Homo sapiens* now have brains at least twice the size of a primate of equivalent body build. The departure of brain size from the allometric line is known as the encephalisation quotient (EQ). Some values for the great apes and early hominids are shown in Table 7.1.

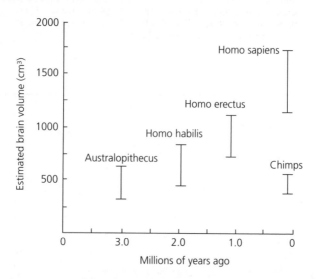

Figure 7.5 Growth in human brain volume during human evolution. Note that during this period body weight also grew but at a slower rate than brain volume. After Deacon, T.W., 'The human brain', in S. Jones *et al.* (eds) *The Cambridge Encyclopaedia of Human Evolution*, 1992, Cambridge University Press

Table 7.1 **Body weights, brain weights and encephalisation quotients (EQ) for selected apes and hominids**

Species	Body weight (g)	Brain weight (g)	EQ[A]
Pongo pygmaeus (orang-utan)	53,000	413	1.07
Gorilla gorilla (gorilla)	126,500	506	0.68
Pan troglodytes (common chimp)	36,350	410	1.41
Homo habilis	40,500	631	2.00
Homo erectus	58,600	826	1.98
Homo sapiens	65,000	1330	2.95

Data from Boaz and Almquist (1997) and other sources.

$$EQ^a = \frac{\text{Actual brain weight}}{\text{Predicted brain weight from } 0.099 \text{ (body weight)}^{0.76}}.$$

(For the mathematically inclined): calculate the EQ for a gibbon

The relevant data are:

Body weight 12.6 kg

Brain weight 0.126 kg

Progress exercise

It is difficult to judge how much weight to attach to the concept of encephalisation when estimating intelligence. One reason is that intelligence is likely to be far too complex to have a simple relationship with the EQ. This is illustrated by what Deacon (1997) has called the 'chihuahua fallacy'. Small dogs such as chihuahua and Pekinese are highly encephalised; that is, they have brains much larger than expected for their body size. The reason is that they have been deliberately bred for smallness in body size, but since brain size is far less variable the breeding programme that led to small dogs has left them with relatively larger brains. In humans the condition of dwarfism also yields high EQs. The best way to explain both these conditions is using the concept of negative somatisation (see Figure 7.3). The point to note is that human dwarves or chihuahuas are not noticeably more intelligent than their normal-sized counterparts. Reviewing the evidence, Deacon concludes that the high EQs of humans are not the result of negative somatisation. In fact, the fossil record shows that hominid body size has been increasing over the last 4 million years.

The puzzle of human intelligence is illuminated to some degree by a comparison between humans and their nearest relatives, the great apes. The term nearest relative means the species with which we most recently shared a common ancestor. On this basis we are more closely related to chimpanzees (Figure 4.2) than monkeys since our last common ancestor with the former was about 6 million years ago and with the latter group about 26 million years ago. Figure 7.6 illustrates this point.

There has been much discussion on how to calculate EQs and their interpretation but whatever measure or formula is used humans always come out on top. We may have once shared a common ancestor with the apes shown in Figure 7.6, but in terms of brain size we left them behind millions of years ago. This may be reassuring for human vanity, but we now have to explain why such an expensive and risky organ should have evolved to such dimensions. There are really two questions here and answering the first helps with the second: the first is why primates evolved larger brains than other mammals; the second is why among our own ancestors did brain size increase well beyond that typical of other primates. These topics are addressed in the next chapter.

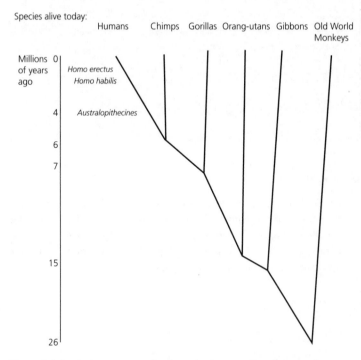

Figure 7.6 **Evolutionary tree of selected primates. The diagram shows that the closest living relatives of humans are chimpanzees**

Summary

- Modern taxonomy (classification systems) places humans in the order of primates and in the family Hominidae, along with chimps and gorillas.
- Humans have larger brains than expected for a primate of our size. This is sometimes expressed as the encephalisation quotient.
- Brain size has increased dramatically in the hominid **lineage** over the last 4 million years of evolution.
- The metabolic requirements of large brains, the necessary premature birth of human babies and the consequent need for prolonged infant care would have favoured increasingly monogamous sexual relationships between our ancestors in the **environment of evolutionary adaptation (EEA)**.

Review exercise

By looking back over the previous chapter, write brief definitions of each of the following terms or concepts:

Hominid   Encephalisation
Australopithecines   Encephalisation quotient
Allometry

Further reading

Jones, S., Martin, R. and Pilbeam, D. (eds) (1992). *The Cambridge Encyclopaedia of Human Evolution*. Cambridge, UK: Cambridge University Press. Numerous experts have contributed to this book. Thorough and well illustrated with plates and diagrams. Excellent for comparing human and primate evolution.

8

The evolution of intelligence

Origins of primate intelligence
Food or sociality: testing the theories
Other theories of the evolution of intelligence
Summary

Origins of primate intelligence

We should remind ourselves that it will not do to say casually that big brains give rise to intelligence, which is obviously useful to survival. If it were this simple all creatures would have big brains. What we need to understand is why a few species of primates accelerated away from the others in terms of brain capacity about 3 million years ago. To understand this it is useful at first to examine primate intelligence. There are two popular theories at present that address the problem of why primates are vastly more intelligent than most mammals. One is that the environment of primates poses special problems in terms of the mental capacity needed to gather food; the other is that group living for primates requires considerable mental skill and agility. We will describe the reasoning behind each theory in turn and then move to examine how these theories and others can be tested.

Environmental factors: foraging behaviour and primate intelligence

Horses and cattle are not renowned for their great intelligence. With their style of life they hardly need to be: they subsist on low-calorie foodstuff in the form of grass, something that is not intellectually demanding to gather. Such animals need large guts to contain the bacteria needed to help break down the cellulose and they need to spend considerable time grazing. Apart from the great apes, most primates are too small to have sufficient gut to ferment large quantities of cellulose and have evolved instead to seek out a more varied diet. Many species are, in effect, unspecialised vegetarians, and, at least for some species, obtaining a balanced diet can be intellectually challenging.

Obtaining food can be broken down into a series of stages:

- Travelling.
- Identification.
- Extraction.

For primates that rely on high-calorie foods, such as fruits, there may only be a few fruit trees in season in a large patch of forest. Remembering where they are is difficult and there is ample evidence to show that primates have effective cognitive maps to help them remember the location of the fruit and the best route between the trees (Garber, 1989). Identification of food requires a good perceptual system and it is significant that unlike many other mammals primates have good colour vision. Extracting food is also taxing. Among the non-human primates, only chimps seem to regularly use tools for food extraction, such as deliberately fashioned twigs to catch insects, or stones to break nuts. Food availability is distributed in time as well as space. Nutritious buds, young leaves or ripe fruit may appear on any one species of plant for a short amount of time only. Large primates cannot afford to specialise and rely on only one or two species of plant for their diet. This, together with the seasonality of foods, also makes significant intellectual demands.

Social factors: machiavellian intelligence and the theory of mind

In recent years there have emerged several related hypotheses suggesting that it may be the demands of the social world that have driven up brain size. These ideas are often grouped together in what Whiten and Byrne (1988) have called the 'machiavellian intelligence hypothesis' – named after the Renaissance politician and author Niccolò dei Machiavelli. The essence of the machiavellian intelligence hypothesis is that primate intelligence allows an individual to serve his or her own interests through a mixture of cunning, deceit and cheating without arousing the suspicions of the group. The analogy with human politics is clear: the successful, cynical and corrupt politician uses his or her position to further his or her own ends while to all appearances serving the people.

In relation to the machiavellian intelligence hypothesis a body of evidence is now beginning to emerge to suggest that some animals are capable of deceiving others. This may not sound like a great intellectual feat but in the animal kingdom only humans and a few other primate species seem to have this ability. Deception requires considerable brain power since an animal intent on doing it needs to understand how the world might appear to another individual, in other words to appreciate the perspective of others. Understanding the mind of another, and realising that other individuals have viewpoints, interests and beliefs, is sometimes called the 'theory of mind'.

Theory of mind was a term first used by primatologists when they realised that chimps could solve problems that depended on them appreciating the intentions of another individual. We can conceive of this appreciation of other minds in terms of orders of intensionality. A daffodil probably has zero-order intensionality: it may wave a pretty flower at us but it is not aware of its own existence – there is no one at home. Self-awareness indicates first-order intensionality. Second-order intensionality involves self-awareness and the realisation that others are similarly aware. From here on it gets ever more complicated: 'I think' is first order, 'I think you think' is second order, 'I think that you think that I think' is third order and so on. Children acquire second-order intensionality between 3 and 4 years. Most adults can keep track of about five or six orders of intensionality before we forget who is thinking what. No wonder the expression 'Oh what a tangled web we weave when first we practice to deceive' is so apt.

It is easy enough to conclude that plants and machines have zero-order intensionality but much harder to decide what has self-awareness or first-order intensionality. **Behaviourism**, a branch of psychology pioneered by Watson in the 1930s and Skinner in the 1950s that supposed that psychologists should concentrate on the outward manifestations of behaviour rather than reports of inner experiences or evolutionary origins, faced this difficulty by treating all animals as machine-like, and so assumed zero-order intensionality. Some even applied this approach to humans, but with limited success.

The important question is whether non-human primates have either first- or second-order intensionality. Byrne and Whiten have concluded that the observational evidence demonstrates that only chimpanzees, orang-utans and gorillas practise intentional tactical deception. Only these apes, in other words, are capable of manipulating the mind of another animal into a false set of beliefs – something requiring second-order intensionality (Byrne, 1995).

So here is the social complexity hypothesis for the growth of primate and then human intelligence. The complex social lives of primates require that they understand their own minds and the minds of others in order to further their own interests. As this became increasingly important to the reproductive success of primates so brain size increased. Against the promise held out by research into the social world of primates we must balance the fact that not everyone is convinced by the idea that some primates have second-order intensionality. Tomasello and Call, for example, conclude 'there is no solid evidence that non-human primates understand the intentionality or mental states of others' (Tomasello and Call, 1997, p. 340).

These reservations, however, do not invalidate the whole social complexity hypothesis. Whatever means chimps use to navigate the complex currents of their social world, it is clear that living in groups makes significant cognitive demands in addition to the demands of finding food and physical survival. These two sets of factors – environment and sociality – may have been inextricably linked in the growth of human intelligence. Some recent work has tested the competing claims of the two theories and does suggest one set of factors may have been crucially important. The next section examines this issue.

Food or sociality: testing the theories

Methodological problems

To test these two competing theories of brain enlargement we obviously need some way of measuring three things:

1. The level of environmental complexity associated with different foraging strategies.
2. The level of social complexity set by group size and group dynamics.
3. The level of intelligence possessed by species that forage and by species that live in groups.

It turns out that there are problems in tackling each of these measurements and we must be aware of the assumptions that need to be made.

Measuring environmental complexity

The cognitive demands of feeding are obviously related to the type of food consumed, in particular its distribution in time and space, its ease of identification and the processing needed before it can be eaten.

Measuring social complexity

The social complexity of a group is indicated somewhat by the mean size of the group: the larger the group the more relationships there are to keep track of and take into account in machiavellian manoeuvres. Measuring group size is also fairly easy and reliable data exists for a range of primate species. We need to be careful, however, since it does not follow that social complexity is linearly related to group size.

Measuring intelligence

Estimating the intelligence of animals is difficult. It is all too easy to be anthropomorphic and assess the cleverness of an animal by how well it performs tasks that humans have designated as clever. Given the controversy surrounding the construction of a fair and culture-neutral IQ test for humans, it is not surprising that there is considerable disagreement over the creation of a 'species-fair' behavioural measure of intelligence.

Faced with the problems of measuring and interpreting intelligent behaviour, we could employ indirect methods. In fact, we already resorted to this when we concluded that the high intelligence of primates is something to do with their deviation above the allometric line of body weight and relative brain size for mammals, in other words their EQ (see Chapter 7).

Brain size and primate diet

Within primates there are differences in feeding behaviour and habitat and if ideas linking foraging and intelligence are correct then it should follow that primate species most dependent on patchy and dispersed (spatially and temporally) foods should show more cerebral development than those reliant only on more uniform resources. Milton (1988) tested these ideas using two contrasting species: howler monkeys (*Alouatta palliata*) and spider monkeys (*Ateles geoffroyi*). Both these species eat leaves and fruit but howlers are more folivorous (leaf eating) than spider monkeys, while spider monkeys are more frugivorous (fruit eating) than howlers. One consequence of this is that spider monkeys have to deal with a food supply area 25 times as large as that of howler monkeys.

When these two species are compared, there are several features that suggest spider monkeys are more intelligent than howler monkeys. The social behaviour of spider monkeys seems to be more complex and they show a greater range of facial expressions than howler monkeys. Perhaps more crucially, the brain sizes of the two species are markedly different (Table 8.1).

Table 8.1 shows that even after body size effects are controlled for (using the EQ values), spider monkeys have twice the brain capacity of howler monkeys.

Table 8.1 Comparison of brain sizes of howler and spider monkeys			
Species	Body weight	Brain weight	EQ
Howler (*Alouatta palliata*)	6.2	50.3	0.66
Spider (*Ateles geoffroyi*)	7.6	107	1.2
Data cited in Milton (1998); EQs calculated from formula given in Chapter 7.			

Milton is generally sceptical about the notion that primate intelligence is related to social complexity:

> Data sets on primates, small mammals, bats and marine mammals therefore suggest that diet (and complexities associated with its procurement) show an association with relative brain size. Little support is found for the view that social systems or breeding systems have a similar effect on brain size. (Milton, 1988, p. 298)

Intelligence and the neocortex

So far we have focused on gross measures of brain size relative to body mass to calculate the EQ for species of primate. There has been the underlying assumption that the EQ must be related directly to intelligence. The EQ, although obviously a better measure than simple brain weight, does not take account of different shapes of brain or differences in brain structure. In fact, there are reasons for suspecting that brain size relative to body mass specified by an EQ value may be only a rough measure of animal intelligence and that we need something more precise.

As long ago as 1970, Maclean argued that the human brain can be divided into three main sections: a primitive core that we have inherited from our reptile-like ancestors; a mid section that contains areas concerned with sensory perception and integrating bodily functions; and, finally, an outer layer or cortex that is distinctive to mammals (Figure 8.1). The word 'cortex' comes from the Latin for bark and it is this crinkly outer layer that lies like a sheet over the cerebrum. It consists largely of nerve cell bodies and has a grey appearance – hence the phrase 'grey matter' to distinguish it from the white matter beneath. In non-primate mammals it accounts for about 35% of the total brain volume. In primates, this proportion rises from about 50% for small monkeys to about 80% for humans. If we are looking for some objective measure of animal intelligence it could be the cortex that we need to concentrate on.

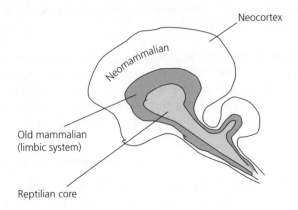

Figure 8 .1 **Triune model of the brain as proposed by MacLean (adapted from MacLean, 1972)**

- **Reptilian core**. Area responsible for basic drives, repetitive and ritualistic forms of behaviour. Involved in 'innate' disposition to establish hierarchies. Also possibly storage of learnt forms of behaviour.
- **Old mammalian (limbic system)**. Contains a number of areas concerned with fighting, feeding, self-preservation, sociability, and affection for offspring.
- **Neomammalian (neocortex)**. Relatively recent in evolutionary time. Well-developed neocortex found only in higher mammals. Receives information from eyes, ears and body wall. Responsible for higher mental functions – well developed in primates, especially humans.

Environmental and social complexity and neocortex volume

MacLean's model is clearly an oversimplification, but if we accept that it may be the neocortex that is the advanced region of the brain concerned with consciousness and thought then it is this region of the brain that should correlate with whatever feature has driven the increase in intelligence in humans and other primates.

To test these competing theories, Robin Dunbar (1993) of the University of Liverpool plotted the ratio of the volume of neocortex to the rest of the brain (i.e. neocortex volume/total brain volume) against various measures of environmental complexity and also against group size. The results were revealing. He found no relationship between neocortex volume and environmental complexity, but a strong correlation between the size of the neocortex and group size (Figure 8.2). This is, of course, so far just an association: the fact that group size rises as neocortex volume does not by itself imply that one caused the other. All we can say at this stage is that the correlation is consistent with the idea that it may be the demands of group living that brought about the growth of brain size in hominids and other primates.

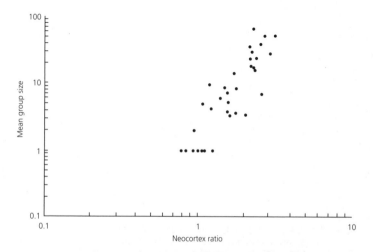

Figure 8.2 **Plot of group size against neocortex ratio for various species of primates. Adapted from Dunbar, R., 'Co-evolution of neocortical size, group size and language in humans', 1993,** *Behavioural and Brain Sciences*, **with permission from Cambridge University Press**

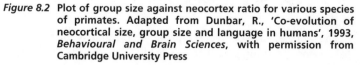

Neocortex and intelligence

The correlation observed in Figure 8.2 looks promising for the machiavellian hypothesis but neocortex volume is still an indirect measure of intelligence. In an attempt to establish whether neocortex ratio correlates with machiavellian intelligence in a more direct way, Byrne and Whiten collected data on actual observed instances of machiavellian intelligence in action. If one primate deceives another in such a way that it shows some appreciation of the mental state of another, then this is taken as an example of machiavellian intelligence. Byrne and Whiten used a tactical deception index which took into account the fact that some primates have been studied more than others. They were also rigorous in excluding episodes that could be reasonably interpreted in other ways (Byrne, 1995). The result is shown in Figure 8.3.

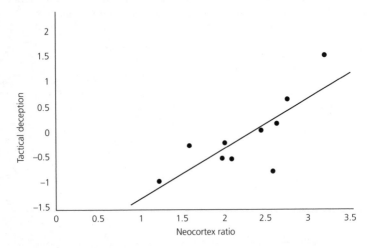

Figure 8.3 **Relationship between neocortical ratio and index of tactical deception for a variety of primates. From Byrne, R.,** *The Thinking Ape,* **1995, by permission of Oxford University Press**

The work of such people as Dunbar, Byrne and Whiten suggests that it is the social complexity of primate life that may have demanded an increase in brain size and we may reasonably infer that this was also probably a powerful factor in driving up the size of brains in early hominids.

Problems with foraging and machiavellian theories

The relationship between group size and intelligence proposed by theorists of the machiavellian school is not without its problems. One serious anomaly is that if it was the demands of a complex social life that drove up intelligence then we should expect those species of primates that are intelligent to live in complex social groups. Yet it is commonly acknowledged that the most intelligent primates are the great apes (chimps, gorillas and orang-utans). Within these species, however, there is considerable diversity in social structures, from the complex multi-male, multi-female groups of chimps, the uni-male harems of gorillas to the relatively solitary mode of existence of orang-utans. Another problem is that some species of monkeys live in larger groups than those of the great apes. Finally, the neocortical ratio of baboons is greater than that of gorillas yet most observational and laboratory studies seem to show that gorillas are more intelligent than baboons. Only gorillas and chimps have been taught a rudimentary sign language, and only chimps and orang-utans routinely use tools.

Against the ideas of those who suggest food sourcing and processing were the prime movers in brain growth we have the evidence of Dunbar and others noted earlier. In addition, we should note that many bird species, such as jays and marsh tits, have been shown to have highly effective memories when it comes to finding food, yet the brains of these birds are not renowned for their size.

There is clearly some linkage between diet and brain growth in humans. Compared to the other great apes humans have large brains and small guts. The digestive tract of gorillas and orang-utans, for example, is dominated by the colon, whereas in the case of humans it is the small intestine that takes up most space. These differences are easily explained by the fact that long ago humans began to exploit a nutritionally rich and varied diet (fruit, meat, vegetables) needing a large small intestine to absorb the nutrients, compared to the foliar diet of gorillas and orang-utans and its associated need for a large colon.

From this comparison, it is clear that the diet of humans would have been more intellectually taxing to gather than that of the other great apes. But we are still left with the question of which came first. Did the demands of a complex diet stimulate increases in brain size, or did some other factor, such as the problems of social life, drive up brain size and bring about the need to fuel these large brains?

Other theories of the evolution of intelligence

In the previous sections we have reviewed two competing and popular theories for the origins of primate (including human) intelligence. It must not be thought, however, that these are the only theories. In this section we briefly describe some of the other contenders for what is one of the most difficult problems in evolutionary theory: the origins of human intelligence. If there ever will be a consensus on what were the definitive causes of brain enlargement for our ancestors we are still a long way from that goal.

Sexual selection and the evolution of the brain: the display hypothesis

Between about 6 and 3 million years ago our ancestors roamed the African savannah with brains about the size of a modern chimpanzee (450 cm^3). Then 2 million years ago there began an exponential rise in brain volume that gave rise to modern humans with brains of about 1300 cm^3. A tripling of brain size in 3 million years is rapid by evolutionary standards: in terms of brain power the hominids left the other primates standing (or rather walking on all fours). One force that can bring about such rapid change is sexual selection. Recall in Chapter 3 that runaway sexual selection has left the peacock saddled with a most unlikely tail. Geoffrey Miller (2000), an evolutionary psychologist at London University, suggests that a similar process has shaped human brains. In this view humans would have examined potential partners not only to estimate their health, age, fertility and social status but also to appraise their cognitive skills. It is this latter criterion that may have set up a runaway growth in brain size. Miller sees this as beginning with females choosing males that are amusing, inventive and have creative brains. Language accelerates the process since the exchange of information can now be used to judge the suitability of a potential partner. Although brain growth was driven by female choice, both sexes gradually acquired larger brains since brains are needed to decode and appreciate inventive male displays. Miller makes a remarkable and what will prove to be a controversial assertion:

> Males produce about an order of magnitude more art, music and literature . . . than women, and they produce it mostly in young adulthood. This suggests that . . . the production of art, music and literature functions primarily as a courtship display. (Miller, 1998, p. 119)

As you might expect, the display hypothesis is controversial. In its favour we might note that many works of art and creative displays are made by young men and that male pop stars and other cultural icons are extremely attractive to the opposite sex. Perhaps Picasso was aware of this function of art when he said that he 'painted with his penis'. He was speaking metaphorically of course but it is significant that both financially and sexually Picasso was very successful.

Hardware–software co-evolution: the stimulus of language

From Australopithecines to modern *Homo sapiens* brain size has roughly doubled every 1.8 million years. This qualifies it for the term exponential growth: growth whereby a quantity doubles every fixed unit of time. Now 1.8 million years might seem like a long time but biologically the evolution of the brain has been remarkably fast. This is why scientists seeking to understand the phenomenon have looked to 'runaway' or 'positive feedback' models to explain it. The idea of sexual selection is a runaway model: females began by preferring clever brains, which meant that men with such brains left more offspring, including daughters with larger brains who preferred even larger male brains and so on.

This can also be understood as positive feedback – where the effect of a growth in something is to make further growth more likely. You can sometimes hear feedback at concerts if a microphone is placed too near a speaker. An initial small sound is picked up by the micro-phone, amplified and fed to the speaker. The microphone then picks up the sound from the speaker, amplifies it and sends it out with an increased volume. The net result is a runaway effect that leads to an ear-piercing whine.

We can also observe an exponential growth in modern computers. There is a law, called Moore's law, which states that the capacity of the latest computers of a given size doubles every 1.5 years. Amazingly, this law has held good over the last 10 years.

The biologist Richard Dawkins has used this law as a metaphor for a view of brain growth which he calls self-feeding co-evolution (Dawkins, 1998). The reasons why computers have grown in power as they have are probably complex, but one of the driving forces must have been the co-evolution of software and hardware. Improved software puts a pressure on the hardware to keep up; in turn, new hardware gives rise to greater software possibilities and so on. As an example, the mouse (hardware) stimulated the graphical user interface (software), which led to the popular Windows software. So what could have been the software and hardware for brains? Dawkins suggests that the hardware is of course the brain material: the neurons and their connections; for the software a number of candidates suggest themselves, perhaps the most obvious being language.

There is still considerable dispute over the question of when language began but it is easy to imagine how a few grunts and signs would carry advantages that led to those who could utter and decode them out-reproducing their rivals. As language grew in complexity so a premium was placed on larger brains to cope with understanding and emitting the sounds of language. Software (language) and hardware (neurons) were embraced in a sort of spiralling waltz that led to an explosion of brain size – and, incidentally, art, culture and the modern world.

Another hardware change brought about by language has been the descent of the larynx. Humans are unique among primates in having a larynx low in the throat. This adaptation, while making it difficult to eat and talk at the same time (giving rise to numerous cases of death by choking each year), allows a wide range of sounds to be made, thereby allowing modern speech with all its subtleties. Chimps could never be made to speak like humans since their larynx is too high. So here it seems the software of language not only inflated our brains but also drove our larynxes deeper into our throat. Or, to put it more strictly, our ancestors with slightly larger brains and slightly lower larynxes fared better in the struggle for existence than their smaller-brained and higher-larynxed contemporaries, they left more offspring and set the evolution of humans on a path that led to the big-brained, chattering humans of today.

Tool use

One of the most obvious differences between the lives of humans and other primates is the reliance of the former on technology. Imagine some sort of bizarre castaway experiment where humans were forced to live without using tools. Very quickly, you will realise how tools permeate our lives and that without them we would quickly perish. In the wild, tool use has been documented in chimps and some populations of orang-utans. Chimps, for example, have been observed to use twigs to extract ants from their nests and stones to break nuts. However, in both these species tool use seems to be an optional extra rather than something essential for life.

It is to tool use that we might look, then, to explain the growth in human brain capacity. If tool use were an important stimulus to brain growth in our evolutionary lineage, then we would expect some association between the sophistication of tool use at any epoch and the brain size of early hominids during the same period. The chain of cause and effect might be that the use of tools early on for such things as catching and processing foods gave survival advantages. From this beginning, more sophisticated tools (sharper points, straighter spears, etc.) may have brought about even greater rewards. But more sophisticated tools would require larger brains to conceive and construct them. This would have set up a selective pressure for increases in brain size – a case of 'tools maketh the man'. Such views about brain size and the use of tools were common about 40 years ago and have been revived of late in a modified form (Byrne, 1997). In 1959, Oakley argued that:

When the immediate forerunners of man acquired the ability to walk upright habitually, their hands became free to make and manipulate tools – activities which in the first place were dependent on adequate powers of mental and bodily co-ordination, but which in turn perhaps increased those powers. (Oakley, 1959, p. 2)

To test the idea that brain growth through evolution was stimulated by tool use, it obviously behoves the investigator to compare the size of brains with the type of technology practised by early hominids at various periods. Brain size can be estimated by the use of endocasts from fossilised skulls. The construction of endocasts involves pouring some substance that sets inside the hollow cavity of a skull and measuring the volume of the cast that results. The volume thus calculated then needs to be scaled for body mass to obtain a measure of the encephalisation quotient (EQ) – a concept discussed in Chapter 6. The EQ of early hominids can then be compared with the state of tool use at any time. Another point of reference here that is useful is the fact that we have accurate information about brain size and tool use for some modern-day great apes such as chimps and orang-utans.

When such comparisons are made the general thrust of the evidence is to throw doubt on the suggestion that tool use served as a major stimulus to brain growth. The reasons are as follows:

- Early species of the hominid lineage such as *Australopithecus afarensis* that lived about 3.5 million years ago yield higher EQs than modern-day chimps yet no tools have been found at Australopithecine sites. This does not rule out the fact that Australopithecines may have used tools, however, since such tools may have been perishable.
- We begin to find tools in the human record about 2 million years ago associated with the earliest *Homo* species, *Homo habilis*. Such tools, however, are very simple and often amount to no more than a stone broken to reveal a sharp edge. Wynn (1988) argues that these tools show no signs of the concept of symmetry, no evidence of a design held in the mind and then imposed on the raw material. Nothing, in short, that reveals any mental sophistication. Wynn estimates that these primitive tools reveal a tool-making competence similar to the abilities of the great apes today. This is a blow to the tool-making hypothesis of cranial enlargement since such hominids had brains of a significantly larger EQ than modern-day chimps (see Table 7.1).
- A period of rapid brain growth took place during the evolution of *Homo erectus* species between 1.5 and 300,000 years ago. As we might expect if the hypothesis is correct, the tools found associated with these hominids are more regular in shape and size and are more sophisticated, showing, for example, a greater degree of symmetry. One crucial problem, however, is that while brain size grew during this period tool manufacture remained remarkably conservative. The evolution of tool design failed to keep up with increases in intelligence.
- Between 300,000 years ago and the present, brains did grow in volume slightly but the explosion of technological sophistication has been enormous. From the invention of symbolic culture (cave paintings, etc.) about 35,000 years ago, through the Neolithic revolution (invention of agriculture) about 11,000 years ago, to the Internet of today, technology has been transformed exponentially through relatively small changes in brain volume since 300,000 years ago and virtually no changes in volume since 35,000 years ago.

Reviewing the evidence Wynn concludes that:

> Given the evidence of brain evolution and the archaeological evidence of technological evolution, I think it fair to eliminate from consideration the simple scenario in which ability to make better and better tools selected for human intelligence. (Wynn, 1988, p. 283)

We have not yet completely solved the problem of why human brains grew so large, but at least there is the feeling that we have a greater range of ideas, tools and insights than ever before to tackle this enigma (Figure 8.4). Perhaps the final answer will be that it was a complex combination of many factors – ecological, sexual, social, linguistic and technological – that were at work. Further insights may come from the human genome project and neurophysiology: as we understand the functioning of the brain so we can infer backwards to the purposes for which it was 'designed' by natural selection. And once we understand the adaptive value of the different aspects of our mental functions, so we will be closer to knowing why a few distant ape-like

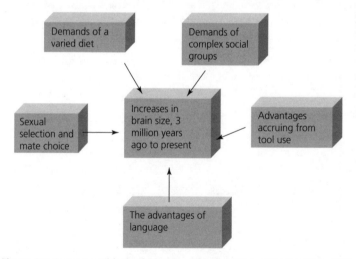

Figure 8.4 **Some possible evolutionary stimuli on the growth of hominid brains**

The chain of cause and effect is likely to be more complex than a one-way influence shown here. Some factors would have interacted with each other and growth in brain size would itself have brought about changes in living conditions

creatures set off on an irreversible track of brain expansion some 4 million years ago. But, perhaps more importantly, we will gain a better understanding of the mind of contemporary humans.

Summary

- The reasons why hominid brains grew so large is a puzzle in evolution. There are a number of competing views:

  (i) The cognitive demands of a varied diet.
  (ii) The role of social factors: the so-called machiavellian hypothesis and the theory of mind.
  (iii) The effects of sexual selection: females (primarily) preferring large-brained mates.
  (iv) The co-evolution of brain tissue (hardware) and language (software).
  (v) The stimulus of tool use.

Review exercise

From the sections above and further reading, compile a table showing how the main theories of brain enlargement stand up in the light of evidence.

Description of theory	Evidence in favour	Evidence against

Further reading

Byrne, R. (1995). *The Thinking Ape*. Oxford: Oxford University Press. A clear exposition of the machiavellian intelligence hypothesis.

Dunbar, R.I.M. (1996). *Grooming, Gossip and the Evolution of Language*. London: Faber & Faber. A readable and popular account of the evolution of brain size and its possible causes.

Miller, G. (2000). *The Mating Mind*. London: Doubleday. A provocative account of the way human sexuality and sexual selection may have been responsible for brain enlargement.

9

Study aids

IMPROVING YOUR ESSAY WRITING SKILLS

At this point in the book you will have acquired the knowledge necessary to tackle the exam itself. Answering exam questions is a skill which this chapter shows you how to improve. Examiners obviously have first-hand knowledge about what goes wrong in exams. For example, candidates frequently do not answer the question which has been set; rather they answer the one that they hoped would come up, or they do not make effective use of the knowledge they have but just 'dump their psychology' on the page and hope the examiner will sort it out for them. A grade 'C' answer usually contains appropriate material but tends to be limited in detail and commentary. To lift such an answer to a grade 'A' or 'B' may require no more than a little more detail, better use of material and coherent organisation. It is important to appreciate that it may not involve writing at any greater length, but might even necessitate the elimination of passages which do not add to the quality of the answer and some elaboration of those which do.

By studying the essays presented in this chapter and the examiner's comments, you can learn how to turn your grade 'C' answer into a grade 'A'. Typically it only involves an extra 4 marks out of 24. Please note that marks given by the examiner in the practice essays should be used as a guide only and are not definitive. They represent the 'raw' marks which would be likely to be given to answers to AQA (A) questions.

In the AQA (A) examination, an examiner would award a maximum of 12 marks for knowledge and understanding (called Assessment Objective 1 – AO1) and 12 marks for evaluation, analysis and commentary (Assessment Objective 2 – AO2). The details of this marking scheme are given in Appendix C of Paul Humphreys' title in this series, *Exam Success in AEB Psychology*, and the forthcoming title *Exam Success in AQA(A) Psychology*. Remember that these are the raw marks and not the same as those given on the examination certificate received ultimately by the candidate because all examining boards are required to use a common standardised system called the Uniform Mark Scale (UMS), which adjusts all raw scores to a single standard across all boards.

The essays given here are notionally written by an 18-year-old in 30 minutes and marked bearing that in mind. It is important when writing to such a tight time limit that you make every sentence count. Each essay in this chapter is followed by detailed comments about its strengths and weaknesses. The most common problems to watch out for are:

- Failure to answer the question but reproducing a model answer to a similar question which you have pre-learned.
- Not delivering the right balance between description and evaluation/analysis. Remember they are always weighted 50/50.
- Writing 'everything you know' about a topic in the hope that something will get credit and the examiner will sort your work out for you. Remember that excellence demands selectivity, so improvements can often be made by removing material which is irrelevant to the question set and elaborating material which is relevant.
- Failing to use your material effectively. It is not enough to place the information on the page but you must also show the examiner that you are using it to make a particular point.

For more ideas on how to write good essays you should consult *Exam Success in AEB Psychology* and the forthcoming title *Exam Success in AQA(A) Psychology* (by Paul Humphreys) in this series.

Practice essay 1

Critically consider the extent to which the theory of sexual selection can explain human reproductive behaviour. (24 marks)

Candidate's answer

The theory of sexual selection was first advanced by Charles Darwin in 1859 and was designed to explain the sexual behaviour of animals. We can explain sexual selection by comparing it with natural selection. In natural selection, the characteristics of an animal are selected according to how well they help it survive and thrive in the natural world. Applied to humans, we might say that natural selection has given us a sweating mechanism in order that we do not overheat.

The theory of natural selection was developed by Darwin over the years 1838–1859. By an amazing coincidence, a naturalist called Alfred Russel Wallace came up with the same theory (near enough) in 1858. He sent a copy of his ideas to Darwin, who then rushed forward his own work on the *Origin of Species*. In my view, the theory of natural selection should be called the Darwin–Wallace theory.

If in natural selection organisms are selected according to their ability to survive and effectively compete for resources in the natural world, in sexual selection it is the member of the opposite sex that does the selecting. In order for an animal to agree to mate it may require some demonstration of fitness or genetic value on behalf of a prospective partner. We can see this with the common peacock. A single female is courted by many males, who display their fine plumage to her.

I think that Darwin's theory is very successful in explaining human sexual behaviour. At a simple level, it explains, for example, why the human sexual urge is so strong. If we did not have strong urges we would not reproduce and we wouldn't be here. Where the theory is particularly successful is in explaining differences between men and women. It is probably fair to say that women are the limiting sex in that men are capable of fathering more babies than a single woman could, over her lifetime, bear. This probably means that men are not naturally monogamous since any man that behaved in a more polygamous way in the past would have left more offspring. Evidence for this comes from a variety of studies. One obvious physical difference between men and women is the fact that men are larger than women are. They are taller and more muscular. This has come about because of sexual selection since in the past (and probably in many cases the present!) men fought other men over access to females. The result of this was that men who were taller and stronger than their rivals did better, giving us the men we see today. Men are only slightly bigger than women are though. Certainly this effect is not so pronounced as found in gorillas, where the male is several times larger than the female and tends to live with the females in a harem situation.

Another physical feature that is illuminating is the size of men's testicles compared to those of other apes. Male chimps have huge testicles and significantly their mating system can be described as promiscuous. In these conditions, a male who is able to produce a lot of sperm is likely to become the father of the offspring of the female. The testicles of gorillas are tiny – even smaller than male humans despite the fact that gorillas are larger. This is interesting since once a male has established his authority over other males and enjoys exclusive access to the females it is of no use to produce large amounts of sperm. Hence, there is no need for large testicles. All this falls under the heading of sperm competition theory. Human males lie somewhere in between.

Another application of Darwinian theory is mate choice and mate preferences. Men place a lot of value on youth and beauty in a prospective partner. The reason for this is that women are only fertile between the ages of about 13 and 45. It is important therefore for men to be sexually attracted to young women. We can ascertain preferences by issuing questionnaires to people or by looking at the advertisements in the personal columns of newspapers. When such studies are done, they tend to reveal that women often prefer high-status males who are wealthy. This is a good adaptive strategy since the best way a woman can increase her reproductive success is to find a male who has good genes and who can provide resources to help look after her children.

If we argue that men are not naturally 100% monogamous then it follows that women are not either. It takes two to tango and if men are mating with more than one woman then women must be mating with more than one man. It could be that women are shopping around for good genes. This occurs in other animals too such as the common hedge sparrow or dunnock, where a female may at first sight appear mono-gamous but secretly she is soliciting 'extra pair copulations'. In human terms, this would be called adultery and studies do show that adultery by both the wife and the husband is a common cause for divorce.

The first paragraph shows that the candidate has a rough grasp of the theory of sexual selection. It was mentioned by Darwin in 1859 but really it was more fully developed in his book of 1871 called *The Descent of Man and Selection in Relation to Sex*. This slight inaccuracy is not a grave fault, however. The comparison with natural selection is useful and helps demonstrate that the candidate does know the difference.

The second paragraph, although factually accurate and interesting, is not relevant to the answer and is ignored by the examiner.

The statement in the third paragraph that sexual selection is all about the opposite sex 'selecting' is reasonably accurate but would have been improved by distinguishing between the process of selection that goes on now when mates choose each other and the historical process of selection that over long periods has brought about change. So, for example, competition between members of one sex (often males) has led to changes in the males that fall under the heading of sexual selection. This has often resulted in males being larger than females or the possession by males of specialised fighting equipment such as tusks, horns or claws. The candidate does appreciate this in the last sentence of the fourth paragraph. The answer would have been clearer if sexual selection had been divided into inter- and intrasexual selection. The example of the peacock is appropriate to illustrate intersexual selection. The answer would have been improved at this point if humans were brought into the discussion. There is a danger here of ignoring the central thrust of the question, which is towards human behaviour.

The answer from the fourth paragraph onwards contains a good mix of reasoning and evidence. There is mention of reproductive rates, testicle size, body size dimorphism, comparisons with the great apes (chimps and gorillas), and studies based on questionnaires and advertisements. The theory of sperm competition is also brought to bear.

While all this scores credit an examiner would expect a more balanced answer for full marks. One of the key phrases in the question is 'critically consider'. This means that the candidate needs to weigh up the success of the theory. An obvious way to do this is to look at the areas where the theory works, the areas where it still has problems and then make some summary judgement. This candidate's answer is a little one-sided in that it is assumed that the theory is entirely successful. Some obvious examples where Darwinian approaches struggle would be homosexual behaviour; the decisions made by some people to remain celibate; decisions made by some couples not to have children; or some weird sexual practices (not too graphic please) that are nothing to do with reproductive success.

The candidate also mentions in the fourth paragraph evidence from a 'variety of studies' which shows that the answer is informed; it would have been improved by quoting names or dates. The candidate uses the comparison with chimps and gorillas appropriately and concludes that 'humans lie somewhere in between'. The answer would have been improved here by driving home the main point, which is that this evidence seems to indicate that humans have not recently evolved in promiscuous groups (such as found among chimps) nor did they emerge from harem (uni-male, multi-female) groups. At this point it would have been useful to stress the fact that although men are capable of fathering many children, babies at birth need prolonged care and it would also have been in the interests of early human males to stay with their spouse and help rear their offspring. Women are also continually sexually receptive (they do not have oestrus cycles like chimps or gorillas) and this tends to reinforce a monogamous bond.

There is a tendency for the answer to be couched in terms of the reproductive interests of men although the last paragraph does restore the balance. The fact that men produce large qualities of sperm (about 3×10^8 per ejaculate) has been used by sperm competition theorists (e.g. Baker and Bellis) to argue that women are also disposed to mate with more than one partner at any time.

This candidate clearly understands natural and sexual selection and can apply these ideas to human behaviour. One problem with the answer is that the candidate is not critical enough of the application of the theory. Problems in applying the theory to humans could have been included.

The mark here would be 8 marks for description and 7 marks for evaluation, giving15/24 and a grade B answer.

Practice essay 2

Describe and evaluate evolutionary accounts of mental disorders. (24 marks)

Candidate's answer

The traditional way to explain mental disorders has been to look at problems in the upbringing of an individual or shocks and traumas in their lives. However, Darwinian psychologists are now beginning to show that evolution may also explain the origin of some disorders. One point in favour of this is that many mental disorders have a genetic basis. Schizophrenia, for example, seems to occur in about 1% of all people irrespective of which culture they belong to. Furthermore, if you have a relative who suffers from this condition you are much more likely than average to develop the condition yourself. If your brother or sister is schizophrenic then you have about a 1 in 10 chance of becoming so yourself. This is not conclusive proof that there is a gene for schizophrenia, however, since brothers and sisters are often reared under the same conditions. More compelling evidence would come from identical twins that are raised apart. We should also realise that simple genetic determinism is not at work here since although you have a 0.1 chance of developing schizophrenia if your sibling has the condition you do in fact share half of your genes with your brother or sister. If it were only a matter of genetics then you would have a 0.5 chance of developing schizophrenia.

If we do accept that there is some genetic basis, however, the problem for evolutionary theory then becomes to explain why these genes are still around. Surely, genes that are bad for us should have been eliminated by natural selection.

The answer to this conundrum may be that even genes that are in some way bad for us may in other ways confer some survival advantage. Sickle-cell anaemia is the classic example of this. It is a condition that has a genetic basis and yet genes for it are still present, particularly in African populations. Why the gene survives is probably that possession of just one copy of the gene can give the carrier some resistance to malaria. It is harder to see, however, what are the advantages of schizophrenia. Usually the sufferers have fewer children than normal. The answer may be that schizophrenia gives people creative abilities that helped their relatives to survive in the past. We may be on the wrong track, however, in looking for a gene 'for' schizophrenia. Although there are high concordance rates amongst relatives it could be that they share a gene for something that disposes them to be more sensitive to environmental causes of schizophrenia rather than a gene for the condition itself.

Another approach is to view mental disorders as extreme manifestations of fears and anxieties that we all experience from time to time. From evolutionary thinking it should follow that we fear the things that are bad for us or perhaps were once hazardous to us in our evolutionary past. As an example, many people fear snakes. This would have been (and still is) an appropriate response in the environment of our evolutionary adaptation (EEA) since snakes were dangerous to primates. Another example is fear of heights. It is not a good idea to be very high off the ground since falling could cause a lot of damage. It is interesting to note that such fears often cause a freezing reaction – this is a sensible response since not moving means you are less likely to fall. Of course, not moving also means you are not able to get down so there are negative effects as well. A better illustration may be that fear brings about physiological changes that could help the organism survive in the face of danger. The release of adrenaline and the increase in heart rate both serve to prepare the body for appropriate action.

Anxieties are like fears in that they cause us to think more carefully about our behaviour to make sure we are not going to damage ourselves. It could be said that fear and anxiety are the price of the entrance ticket to the human race. They may not always be enjoyable but without them we wouldn't have evolved to our current position. The problem with all this of course is that some people have extreme fears, phobias, or experience irrational anxiety. Some people have a fear of birds, for example, yet it is hard to see how birds represent a real risk to us today or in the past. The other problem with this approach is to explain why some people but not all experience extreme versions of fears such that they become phobias. This shows that evolutionary reasoning may not be the only answer.

Another way in which evolution could help us understand mental disorders is by showing that our modern environments (big cities, jet travel, fast food and so on) are out of step with our genes that were designed for past environments. To take a physical example, obesity was probably not a great problem that our Stone Age ancestors had to deal with. In the past people had to run to catch their dinner and what they caught would certainly not be high in fats and sugars. Yet, our modern way of life allows people to eat too much food of dubious quality. Applying this to mental disorders it could be that we are not well adapted to modern life and so problems result.

Examiner's comments

Notice that the key words in the question are describe and evaluate. Equal marks will be available for each of these tasks. This means that the candidate must show an understanding of how evolutionary theory tackles mental disorders as well as evaluating the success of the programme so far. The candidate here does show that he/she is capable of both. The descriptive part has some breadth although more evolutionary angles could have been discussed. This is a pity since most candidates find description easier than evaluation. Here the evaluation is well argued with lots of commentary and contrasting views embedded in a discussion. Schizophrenia, for example, is used as an effective illness to illustrate the problem of seeking genes that cause it. Concordance studies are used to show that there is a genetic basis to schizophrenia although this is suitably qualified since we have not identified the genes responsible. The issue of why maladaptive genes survive is tackled and the example of sickle-cell anaemia is used to good effect.

In the fifth paragraph, the candidate introduces another evolutionary approach. This part would have been improved by giving the approach a name, either the 'genome lag' or 'exiles from Eden hypothesis'. The answer at this stage would also have been improved by some evaluation of this view. For example, if our genes are so out of kilter with modern lifestyle how come, in population terms, are we doing so well? There are 6 billion humans on the planet compared to about 250,000 of our nearest relative, the common chimp. The answer could have been made better by expanding on the phrase 'problems result'. What sort of problems and what evidence is there that they have resulted? The student could have critically considered, say, depression and evaluate the extent that the epidemic of depression may be the result of patterns of life (e.g. break-up of kin support units and networks) to which we are not constitutionally suited.

The answer could have been improved by a consideration of other ways that evolutionary theory tackles disorders such as inclusive fitness theories or the social homeostasis or rank theories of depression. The candidate would also have gained more credit if specific studies had been quoted and considered. Finally, a comparison of the evolutionary approach with other approaches would help the student score more evaluation points since it could be demonstrated that other approaches (e.g. behaviourism) also offer convincing accounts of the origin of mental disorders.

Total: 9 marks for description and 7 for evaluation, giving 16/24 and a grade B answer.

Practice essay 3

Describe and evaluate attempts to explain the evolution of human intelligence. (24 marks)

Candidate's answer

To explain the evolution of intelligence we need to do two things: (a) explain what intelligence is and (b) show that the high intelligence possessed by humans has some adaptive function and therefore has helped humans to survive and reproduce.

If we take intelligence to consist of problem-solving ability, use of language and effective use of memory, then all of these things can be found in other animals. Chimpanzees and even rats can be trained to solve problems to find food. Language has been successfully taught to apes – although this has to be sign language since the vocal cords of apes are not suited to human language – and the fact that animals can navigate shows that they have the ability to memorise routes. Despite the fact that other animals obviously possess intelligence of sorts, it is humans who possess it in abundance. In terms of language, problem-solving ability and brain size in relation to body size, humans outstrip all other creatures. But why did our brains grow so large?

There is as yet no universally accepted answer to this question, but there are many plausible theories. One is that primates need large brains in order to cope with the demands of finding food. Another is that primates live in social groups and hence need large brains to be able to satisfy their own interests and desires while at the same time working cooperatively with others. This last hypothesis is sometimes called the machiavellian theory of mind. In this model, humans develop large brains to enable them to deceive others and monitor the intentions of others. This theory is closely allied with the theory of mind, which suggests that an important intellectual skill, possibly unique to humans, is the ability to appreciate the perspective (the mind) of others.

Another theory is that sexual selection drove up the size of brains. This theory suggests that the human brain may be like the peacock's tail in that it has grown enormously large because of the force of sexual selection. A sort of runaway effect would be set up if women preferred men with large brains.

One idea that used to be popular but is now largely dismissed is the idea that standing upright (bipedalism) was the step that promoted large brain growth. Once humans stood upright, the argument goes, then their field of view would be greater, running and throwing become easier and large brains are now selected for. The problem with this is that some early species of hominids stood upright but rapid brain growth did not follow this event.

The final theory is that brain and language evolved together. As soon as language emerged it would demand a lot of brain capacity; as brain capacity grew to cater for this so language became more sophisticated. Language ability would be selected for since being able to talk would bring great reproductive advantages.

However, high intelligence and large brain size bring its own problems. To enable human heads to pass through the pelvic canal at birth babies have to be born premature. This enables brain growth to take place outside of the womb after birth. The trouble with this is that babies are then very dependent on care from their parents. Babies are very vulnerable and so too the risks to the mother at childbirth are high. It is as if evolution made us pay a terrible price for our large heads. This shows of course that large brains must have once carried great survival advantages to outweigh these losses at birth. This brings us back again to what these survival advantages were. Some have suggested the ability to make tools; others have suggested that throwing things to bring down prey required sophisticated computing ability.

Examiner's comments

The answer begins with a useful and valid way of posing the problem.

The second paragraph gains a little credit for evaluation. The point about definition of intelligence is appropriate and it is true that other animals have cognitive skills, but the student does not draw a conclusion from this in relation to the question. The student also does not point out that attempts to teach apes language have not succeeded in producing anything more than very basic sentences. It is not clear that other animals construct memory maps in very complex ways. The last sentence of this paragraph brings us back, thankfully, to answering the question.

The answer would have been improved by some commentary on the fact that brain size and its growth during the evolution of the hominid line are used as a proxy for intelligence. Some information about the size of human brains in comparison to other primates and the growth in brain size over the last 2 million years of hominid evolution would have been appropriate. This would have then led to an evaluation of whether it is brain size overall or part of the brain (e.g. the neocortex) that most strongly correlates with intelligence.

The third paragraph tackles the question head on. The two basic theories are mentioned – finding food and living in groups – but not much detail is given as to why these should be intellectually demanding. The phrase 'machiavellian theory of mind' is a conflation of the machiavellian intelligence hypothesis and theory of mind. They are linked ideas but this conflation does tend to indicate that the student is not really aware of the difference. The answer would be improved by a more explicit consideration of the problem of group living, particularly such things as remembering favours and avoiding deception, and how these may have stimulated brain growth.

Similarly, the point about sexual selection in paragraph five gains some credit as an idea that has been advanced by some evolutionary psychologists, but more depth would have been useful. The student could have pointed to problems with the theory such as why women also have large brains and hence have scored more on evaluation.

The fifth paragraph scores some credit for evaluation. The student considers bipedalism and dismisses it with hard evidence about bipedalism and brain growth in the evolutionary record. This bit of the answer would have been improved if the student had named the Australopithecines as the hominid species that acquired bipedalism without a following increase in brain capacity.

The language–brain co-evolution is briefly described although it lacks the concept of feedback. The final paragraph is slightly tangential to the question asked, although it is accurate. A little credit is given for the point that whatever the reason why intelligence grew it must have been a good one to outweigh losses of life at childbirth and infant mortality.

Overall, the answer would be much improved by more evaluation. The foraging hypothesis is not evaluated at all. There are some studies showing that primates that seek out a varied and intellectually demanding diet do have larger brains than those whose diet is easier to obtain. Other studies (e.g. Dunbar and Byrne) tend to show that the neocortex part of the brain does not relate to foraging demands. Some good evaluation points could have been scored here. The machiavellian intelligence hypothesis is described, for example, but not evaluated. What is the evidence in its favour? Do any studies throw doubt on this hypothesis? An obvious point to make would be that orang-utans are intelligent primates yet do not live in large groups. In addition, gorillas seem to be about as intelligent as chimps yet their group size is much smaller.

A good theory to cite would have been the idea that tool use stimulated intelligence. Some recent studies seem to show that sophistication in tool use did not coincide with increases in brain size. This would tend to throw doubt on this theory.

Marks: about 10 for description and 4 for evaluation, giving 14/24 and a grade B answer.

KEY RESEARCH SUMMARIES

Article 1

Greenlees, I. A. and McGrew, W. C. (1994). Sex and Age Differences in Preferences and Tactics of Mate Attraction: Analysis of Published Advertisements, *Ethology and Sociobiology*, 15: 59–72.

Aims of Study

This study aimed to test a number of predictions from evolutionary psychology using data from advertisements published in the lonely hearts or personal columns of newspapers and magazines. A total of thirteen hypotheses were tested:

1 Women, more than men, will seek cues to financial security
2 Men more than women will advertise earning potential and resources

3   Women, more than men, will seek mates older than themselves

4   Women, more than men, will ask for an investment in time as a precondition for a relationship

5   Men, more than women, will advertise willingness to invest resources

6   Men, more than women, will seek partners younger than themselves

7   Men, more than women, will seek and value physical appearance

8   Women, more than men, will advertise physical appearance

9   Men, more than women, will reveal hobbies that display resource acquisition, status and earning potential

10   Women, more than men, will disclose hobbies that reveal health and fitness

11   More married, or attached men, will seek extramarital affairs

12   More men, than women, will seek relationships of a casual nature

13   Women, more than men, seek relationships of a long-term monogamous type

Procedures

The study used 1,357 advertisements from the "Eye Love" column of *Private Eye* – a British fortnightly magazine with a readership of about 700,000. The advertisements were taken from issues July 1987–Dec 1989. 375 of these advertisements were rejected on the grounds that they were obscure or, for example, were there to obtain visas. Chi-squared tests were used to examine differences between men and women.

Findings and conclusions

The authors found support for eleven of the thirteen hypotheses. The two hypotheses that were not supported were 9 and 10.

Evaluation

This is an important study because the participants are not consciously taking part in a psychology experiment and so the tendency to behave as the researchers want is not evident. In these cases the advertisement represent real people seeking real partners and not subjects filling in questionnaires. On the other hand we could question the sample used (see discussion points below)

Dicussion points

By responding to the following points you can perform your own evaluation

a) How do the hypotheses 1–13 listed above follow from evolutionary expectations? If you have problems with this re-read Chapters 2, 3 and 4 of this book
b) What problems might there be with the source of the samples? Consider who reads *Private Eye* and the period from which the advertisements were taken. Are the advertisements representative of the population as a whole?
c) Bearing in mind your answer to b) above, how might the study be improved or further evidence collected?
d) Speculate on why hypotheses 9 and 10 were not supported

Article 2

Singh, D. (1993). Adaptive significance of female physical attractiveness: role of waist to hip ratio, *Journal of Personality and Social Psychology*, 65 (2): 293–307.

Aims of Study

In Darwinian psychology that which is perceived as attractive in a potential sexual partner should correlate with the fitness of that partner and his or her reproductive potential. Singh aimed to test this with regard to preferred body shape in male preferences.

Procedures

The indicator of body shape that was chosen was the waist to hip ratio or WHR (that is, the circumference at the waist divided by the circumference at the hips). Singh also trawled the medical literature to find out if the WHR was related in any way to such physiological conditions as fertility, age of onset of puberty and health status. Singh then looked for a correlation between health and fertility of various WHR types from the medical literature and men's preferences for body shape. Men's preferences were elicited by showing subjects line drawings depicting women with various WHRs in three body mass groups: underweight, average, and overweight. A total of 106 American male participants was used (72 white and 34 Hispanic).

Findings and conclusions

Singh found that WHR was a very strong predictor of attractiveness. The preferred WHR for women in all groups was 0.7. This WHR was that also found to be healthy and fertile from the medical literature.

Evaluation

This paper by Singh and his subsequent work testing female preferences has been enormously influential. Some have criticised the work and its methodology and others have sought to take the work further with other subject groups. The work is pioneering in the sense that it provides hard evidence that attractiveness is linked to reproductive fitness. Such a linkage is imperative for Darwinians to establish since it is an axiom that natural selection has shaped our desires and inclinations. By responding to the following discussion points you can perform your own evaluation.

Discussion points

a)   What role may culture play in shaping our preferences? Remember that the participants were Americans subject to massive influences from a highly visual culture.

b)   How could you test if preferences for a WHR of about 0.7 are universal and part of a common and evolved psychological mechanism or are subject to local variation?

Glossary

Adaptation   A feature of an organism that has been shaped by natural selection such that it enhances the fitness of its possessor. Adaptation can also refer to the process by which a particular trait is shaped by the selection of genes responsible for it, so that the trait now appears well designed and fit for its purpose.

Adaptive significance   The way in which the existence of a physical or behavioural feature can be related to the function it served and may continue to serve in helping an animal survive and reproduce.

Allele   A particular form of a gene. There may be many forms of alleles within a population of one species. A gene influencing eye colour, for example, could exist in many different forms or alleles, thereby giving rise to a variety of eye colours in the population. For virtually all traits, a human possesses two alleles: one inherited from the father and one from the mother. An allele is therefore a sequence of nucleotides on the DNA molecule.

Allometry   The relationship between the size of an organism as measured by, for example, length, volume or body mass, and the size of a single feature such as brain size. The relationship can often be expressed by mathematical allometric functions or by graphs showing allometric lines.

Australopithecines   Literally means the 'southern apes'. They were the earliest known hominids, which appeared on the plains of southern Africa about 4 million years ago.

Behaviourism The school of psychology largely founded by Watson and continued by Skinner that suggests that only observable behaviour should be the subject matter of psychology.

Carrier An individual who carries a defective gene (i.e. a specific allele) for a condition (usually a disorder) but who does not display the symptoms of the disorder.

Chromosome Structures in the nucleus of a cell that contain DNA. A chromosome contains DNA and has proteins bound to it.

Coefficient of genetic relatedness (*r*) The probability that an allele chosen at random from one individual will also be present in another individual. It can also be thought of as the proportion of the total genome in one individual present in another as a result of common ancestry; hence the genetic relatedness between yourself and your mother is 0.5 since you have inherited 50% of your genes from her.

Cystic fibrosis A disease that occurs in people who possess two copies of a particular defective allele. Individuals with only one copy are carriers. The symptoms include excessive secretion of mucus into the lungs.

Dishonest signal A sign or signal designed to impress a potential mate or deter a potential rival, but one that falsely advertises the quality of the signaller.

DNA Deoxyribonucleic acid. The molecule that contains the information needed to build cells. The information on DNA is passed to offspring through inheritance.

Environment of evolutionary adaptation (EEA) A concept highly favoured by evolutionary psychologists. That period in human evolution (roughly between 3 million and 35,000 years before the present) during which time the genes carried by humans were shaped and selected by natural selection to solve survival problems operating then.

Fitness The fitness of an organism is a measure of the number of offspring it leaves or is likely to leave. Direct fitness (sometimes called Darwinian fitness) can be thought of as being proportional to the number of genes contributed to the next generation by production of direct offspring. Indirect fitness is related to the number of genes appearing in the next generation by an individual helping kin that also carry those genes. Inclusive fitness is the sum of direct and indirect fitness.

Function The function of a physical or behavioural trait is sometimes used as shorthand for its adaptive value. Hence we may say that the functional reason why women do not ovulate while they are lactating and feeding young is to help both the mother and her existing offspring to survive by avoiding the strain of another pregnancy. Unfortunately, to confuse the psychology student, the word has acquired other meanings. In psychology, functionalism became concerned with how individuals became adapted or adjusted in their own lives rather than how traits that had been selected over time became manifest. The situation is further confused by a modern school of functionalism – a merger of cognitive science and artificial intelligence – that uses the word in terms analogous to mathematical functions where the mind is interpreted in terms of computer-like inputs and outputs.

Gamete A sex cell. Unlike most cells in the human body, gametes only contain one copy of any chromosome. A gamete can be an egg or a sperm.

Gene A unit of hereditary information made up of specific nucleotide sequences in DNA.

Gene pool The entire set of alleles present in a population. Your own genes, for example, form one small part (in volume and variety) of the entire human gene pool.

Genome The entire set of genes carried by an organism.

Genotype The constitution of an individual in terms of the genes they carry.

Genus In classification the genus is the category (taxon) above the level of a species but below that of a family. Hominids (*Homo sapiens*, *Homo erectus,* etc.), for example, belong to the genus *Homo*.

'Good genes' theory An approach to sexual selection that suggests individuals choose mates according to the fitness potential of their genome.

Hominids Modern-day humans and their ancestors in the genus *Homo*.

Honest signal A signal that reliably communicates the quality of an individual in terms of its fitness.

Immune system The complex variety of responses and cells that enable the body to resist disease.

Inbreeding The production of offspring from two individuals who are genetically related to some degree.

Inclusive fitness Fitness that is measured by the number of copies of one's genes that appear in current or subsequent generations in offspring and non-offspring. *See* fitness.

Infanticide   The deliberate killing of an infant shortly after its birth.

Intensionality   A term used to express degrees of self-awareness and the awareness of the mental states of others. First-order intensionality is self-consciousness ('I know'); second-order, the awareness that others may have self-awareness (I know that you know'); third-order, the knowledge that others may be aware of your thoughts (I know that you know that I know) and so on.

Lineage   A sequence showing how species are descended from one another.

Machiavellian intelligence   A type of intelligence that enables individuals to serve their own interests in social situations. One idea is that a factor in the growth of intelligence in primates was the need for an individual to manipulate its social world through a mixture of cunning, deceit and alliances.

Monogamy   The mating of a single male with a single female.

Operational sex ratio   The ratio of sexually receptive males to females in a particular area or over a particular time.

Order   A unit of classification above the family and below the class. Humans belong to the order of Primates.

Ovulation   The release of a female sex cell or ovum (plural: ova) from an ovarian follicle as a prelude to possible fertilisation by sperm from a male.

Paradigm   A cluster of ideas and theories that are consistent and form part of a distinct way of understanding the world. Evolutionary psychology can be regarded as a paradigm.

Parasite   An organism in a relationship with another, called the host, such that the parasite gains in fitness at the expense of the host.

Parental investment   Donation of care and attention to offspring at the expense of a parent's ability to raise future offspring.

Polyandry   A type of mating system such that a single female mates with more than one male in a given breeding season.

Polygamy   A situation where one sex mates with more than one member of the other sex. Polygamy can be simultaneous where an individual has many partners at any one time, or serial where the partners are spread over time.

Polygyny   A mating system whereby a single male mates with more than one female in a given breeding season.

Proximate cause In behavioural terms the immediate mechanism or stimulus that initiates or triggers a pattern of behaviour. The proximate cause of tanning in the sun is the biochemical chain of events leading to the release of melanin in response to sunlight. The ultimate cause is that such a system prevents the skin from further damage and so helps the organism to survive.

Mutation In modern genetics a mutation is a change in the base sequence in the DNA of a genome that can be passed on to the next generation. Most mutations are damaging but occasionally mutations help the individual survive.

Phenotype The characteristics of an organism as they have been shaped by both genes and environmental influences.

Selection The differential survival of organisms (or genes) in a population as a result of some selective force. 'Selectionist' thinking is the approach that seeks to show how the characteristics of an organism can be interpreted as the result of years of selection acting upon its ancestors.

Sexual dimorphism Differences in shape, size, physiology or behaviour between the sexes in a single species.

Sexual selection Selection that takes place as a result of mating behaviour. Intrasexual selection occurs as a result of competition between members of the same sex. Intersexual selection is a result of choices made by one sex for features of another.

Species A species is a set of organisms that possess similar inherited characteristics and, crucially, have the potential to interbreed to produce fertile offspring.

Sperm competition Competition between sperm from two or more males found together in the reproductive tract of the female.

Strategy A pattern of behaviour or rules guiding behaviour shaped by natural selection to increase the fitness of an animal. A strategy does not usually mean a set of conscious decisions, rather a pattern of behaviour that is evoked in response to some stimulus and usually helps the organism survive.

Symmetry A state where the physical features of an organism on one side of its body are matched in size and shape by those on the other. Symmetry may be an indication of physiological health since stress, such as caused by parasite infection, decreases symmetry. Animals may therefore use symmetry as an honest signal of fitness.

Taxonomy The theory and practice of classifying organisms.

Teleology   The belief that nature has purposes, that events are shaped by intended outcomes.

Testis   Male sex organ that produces sperm and associated hormones. Plural: **testes**

Theory of mind   The suggestion that an important component of the mental and emotional life of humans and some other primates is the ability to be self-aware and to appreciate that others also have awareness. Having a theory of mind is an essential component of machiavellian intelligence.

Ultimate explanation   The explanation for the behaviour of an organism that reveals its adaptive value. *See also* proximate.

Answers to progress exercises

Chapter 1

Examples may include: putrefying meat, excrement, some toxic gases.

Proximate: the odours are due to molecules of a gas or vapour that are detected by sensory receptors in the nose. The brain interprets the signal from this as a bad (repulsive) odour.

Ultimate: such odours are often associated with hazards to health (e.g. excrement or bad meat). Genes coded for a response that led to avoidance of these odours and objects tended to survive.

Review exercise

Description/Definition	Term
An account of the cause of something in terms of mechanisms that have developed in the lifetime of an individual, e.g. nervous structures, hormonal effects	Proximate explanation

The sum of the information carried on the genes of an individual	Genotype
The process of selecting out successful genes and allowing unsuccessful ones to become rare or extinct	Natural selection
A group of similar-looking organisms that can interbreed to produce fertile offspring	Species
A sudden and undirected change in the molecular structure of DNA	Mutation
The body of an organism as a result of both environmental and genetic effects	Phenotype
An explanation of some feature of the human mind or body that refers to the way such a feature helped ancestors survive	Ultimate explanation
The process by which organisms evolve to be well suited to their mode of life	Adaptation
A long spiral molecule that carries the information necessary to build cells and bodies	DNA

Chapter 2

Review exercise

In the breeding season northern elephant seals form groups such that one male has exclusive sexual access to several females. The females only mate with this bull male. We can say that the male is polygynous while the females are monogamous.

In Western society the marriage contract is an expression of a monogamous bond. However, adultery is common and often a reason for divorce. A male committing adultery could be said to be behaving polygynously A female committing adultery is displaying polyandry.

From a biological point of view, a harem can be viewed as a mechanism for a ruler to maximise the spread of his genes.

Chapter 3

Honest signal	*Functional (adaptive) significance*
Clothes to emphasise narrow waist	Indicates youth, fertility and the fact that the woman is not pregnant
Tight clothes to emphasise figure: musculature in men, shape in women	Indicates youth, strength
Rolex watch	Indicates wealth (but could be a fake!)
Expensive clothes	Signals wealth and status
Dishonest signal	*Functional (adaptive) significance*
Shoulder pads in a man's suit	Suggests upper body strength and musculature – potentially attractive features to women

Cosmetics	Can disguise the effects of age or heighten perception of size of eyes (indicating youth)
High heels	Emphasises length of legs. Note that length of legs in women is long in proportion to size of body as they approach puberty. Long legs could be a signal of high fertility. In men high heels could serve to emphasise height. Allegedly, Tony Blair uses shoe inserts to increase his apparent stature
Hair dye	When used to disguise grey hair it masks signs of ageing. In creating blonde hair it also could indicate youth since hair darkens with age

Chapter 4

Exercise 1

The number of sperm ejaculated is consistent with sperm competition theory. Chimps ejaculate the largest number, as expected from the high degree of sperm competition that takes place in their multi-male multi-female (promiscuous) mating system. Gorillas ejaculate the least since once a male has secured a harem he has little to fear from rival males. Humans are in between, which suggests we are not polygynous to a high degree. Neither are we adapted to promiscuous mating behaviour

Exercise 2

Q1

(a) Offered: age, petite and slim implies attractiveness. Probably intelligent and well qualified.

(b) Sought: male of some status and wealth, male who is intelligent.

Q2 Could use another person to decide if ad is offering the categories to be examined. Someone who is ignorant of the expectations.

Exercise 3

Q1 Description of differences: largest difference in 30–39 category. Difference decreases with age to 60 and then reverses such that men are more likely to seek resources.

Hypothesis: Resources are relatively more important for women when seeking a lifelong partner, possibly with a view to raising children, in age groups 20–29 and 30–39. Resources are less important for women in the 60–69 category since many women now may be financially secure and children are no longer a consideration. The sex ratio at this age is biased in favour of women (i.e. more women than men in this category) and so men may be able to expect a woman of some substance for a secure old age. Men can 'call the shots'.

Q2 How to test: Examine population statistics on men and women in the 60–69 category. Issue questionnaires to men and women to elucidate wants.

Exercise 4

Q1 The data reveals a number of significant facts:

(a) Women tend to initiate divorce more often than men – totals for both categories are higher for women.

(b) When men do initiate a divorce it is more likely to be on grounds of adultery.

In terms of Darwinian psychology (a) could be explained by the fact that a wrong choice of partner by a woman is more damaging (reproductively) than for a man since women have a shorter period of fertility; (b) is possibly related to the fact that adultery is felt more strongly than bad behaviour by men due to uncertainty of paternity.

Q2

(a) The pattern is that most divorces are initiated by women until the age group >60, when the same number of women as men seek divorce.

(b) A woman is more likely to initiate a divorce early on in a marriage since she must quickly decide who is likely to make a good father. A wrong decision must be quickly corrected if she is to find another male to father her children, or indeed to protect her existing children in the face of male aggression.

Q3 It seems that adultery declines in relative importance for men as a cause of the break-up of a marriage as age increases. This could be because wives are less likely to have adulterous affairs as they age. One reason for this may be that they become less attractive to would-be philandering males, or they are more likely to make a decision when young that the relationship is not working and another must be sought for the reasons given in answer to Q2(b) above.

In addition, adultery may be less important for a man as he ages since he becomes less worried about paternity insecurity as his wife ages.

Review exercise

Differences in body size between males and females are part of a phenomenon called sexual dimorphism. The sex that is the larger of the two can be expected to compete for the smaller sex. This process of intrasexual selection is usually found when mating is polygamous. The fact that human males are slightly larger than females could indicate that males once competed for females. The testes of men are much larger, however, than those of gorillas and this is consistent with the suggestion that humans did not evolve in groups consisting of a single male having exclusive sexual access to a harem of females.

For men paternity confidence is an ever-present problem and they have evolved psychological mechanisms to increase paternity confidence. One of these might be the experience of the emotion of jealousy. Men experience a longer period of fertility than women and can be expected to be preferentially attracted to younger women. Women are predicted to be less concerned about age than men but to look for signs of status and wealth in a potential partner.

Chapter 5

Exercise 1

In this hypothetical scenario, fruit A would probably be regarded as delicious and would be highly sought after. Fruit B would probably taste terrible, possibly provoke vomiting and would be a source of terror to modern humans.

Exercise 2

The landscape seems unsettled; notice the swirling lines that signify a state of inner disquiet. The figures are isolated from each other almost like ghosts. They are expressionless.

Review exercise

Emotion	Possible function
Sexual jealousy	Aggressive control over mate to ensure paternity confidence
Fear of water	Most primates do not like water. Risk of drowning or capture by predator (e.g. reptile)
Delight in the behaviour of young infants	Ensures that care and help is given. Love serves to bond parent to child and ensures that the child is protected.
Laughter when someone has made a particularly clever joke	The uncontrollable release of this emotion shows the other that you have sufficient intelligence to grasp the meaning

Guilt in not returning a favour or helping a friend	The emotion ensures that a favour is returned. This helps the donor and recipient since sharing can sometimes benefit both parties
Disgust at the sight of, say, drinking water contaminated with faecal matter	Risk of disease. The emotion of disgust ensures that the water is not drunk

Chapter 6

Exercise 1

1. (a) About 1%.
   (b) About 5% (from Table 6.3).
2. 15%. This is from $10 \times 1.5\%$, the lambda$_S$ is 10.

Exercise 2

Contrasting states of depression and mania in bipolar depressive disorders

Feature	Depressed state	Mania
Mood	Depressed	Elated
Self-esteem	Low	High
Appearance	Drab and scruffy	Smart and flamboyant
Social manner	Submissive	Domineering
Speech	Slow	Rapid
View of future	Pessimistic	Optimistic
Sexual libido	Reduced	Increased

Review exercise

(a) This is probably related to the genome lag hypothesis. John's biorhythms are programmed for him to sleep at night. Modern civilisation requires that he works during this time. There is therefore a nature/environment mismatch.

(b) This seems to be a case of bipolar depression. There may be a genetic base to this. The fact that such genes persist is illustrated by the fact that Kevin has other talents that may be linked with his mania, i.e. he is creative, intelligent and attractive to the opposite sex.

(c) This could be explained by inclusive fitness theory. Martha unconsciously reasons that the best chance for her genes is now to leave her wealth to her grandchildren. Her own life is steadily consuming her wealth and since she is well past reproductive age it makes genetic sense for her to end her life.

(d) This is an example of the genome lag hypothesis and the adaptive value of phobias. A phobia about height has some adaptive value and James has become conditioned to fear heights through an early experience. The phobia is irrational to some degree. The far greater risk to his life comes from his being overweight; he does not appreciate this, however, since humans probably did not evolve to be easily sensitised to this problem in the environment of evolutionary adaptation. In the distant past food surpluses would be rare. Hence we have taste buds that incline us to over-consume fats and carbohydrates.

Chapter 7

Exercise 1

$EQ = 126g/0.099(12600)^{0.76} g = 126/129.3 = 0.97$

Review exercise

> **Hominid** Early type of human belonging to the genus *Homo*. Our ancestors such as *Homo erectus*, *Homo habilis*.
>
> **Australopithecines** Literally southern apes since they were first discovered in southern Africa. A genus of primates that evolved into hominids.
>
> **Allometry** The way in which the sizes and proportions of an organism scale when different-sized organisms of the same type are compared.
>
> **Encephalisation** The process of brain enlargement.
>
> **Encephalisation quotient** A measure of how large the brain of an organism is compared to other similar organisms or more strictly the size of a brain compared to the allometry of scaling.

References

Allen, N. (1995). Towards a computational theory of depression. *ASCAP: The Newsletter of the Society for Sociophysiological Integration* **8**(7): 3–12.

Baker, R.R. (1996). *Sperm Wars*. London: Fourth Estate.

Baker, R.R. and Bellis, M.A. (1995). *Human Sperm Competition*. London: Chapman & Hall.

Barash, D. (1979). *The Whisperings Within*. New York: Harper & Row.

Baron-Cohen, S., Leslie, A.M. and Frith, U. (1985). Does the autistic child have a 'theory of mind'? *Cognition* **21**: 37–46.

Betzig, L. (1982). Despotism and differential reproduction. *Ethology and Sociobiology* **3**: 209–221.

Betzig, L. (1986). *Despotism and Differential Reproduction: A Darwinian View of History*. Hawthorns, NY: Aldine de Gruyter.

Bevc, I. and Silverman, I. (2000). Early separation and sibling incest: a test of the revised Westermarck theory. *Evolution and Human Behaviour* (21): 151–161.

Birkhead, T. (2000). *Promiscuity*. London: Faber & Faber.

Birkhead, T.R., Moore, H.D.M. and Bedford, J.M. (1997). Sex, science and sensationalism. *Trends in Ecology and Evolution* **12**: 121–122.

Boaz, N.T. and Almquist, J. (1997). *Biological Anthropology*. Englewood Cliffs, NJ: Prentice-Hall.

Bowlby, J. (1969). *Attachment Theory, Separation, Anxiety and Mourning*, vol. 6. New York: Basic Books.

Buss, D. (1989). Sex differences in human mate preferences. *Behavioural and Brain Sciences* **12**: 1–49.

Buss, D. (1994). *The Evolution of Desire*. New York: Harper Collins.

Buss, D. (1996). Sexual conflict: evolutionary insights into feminism and the battle of the sexes. In D.M. Buss and N.M. Malamuth (eds) *Sex, Power and Conflict: Evolutionary and Feminist Perspectives* (pp. 296–318). New York: Oxford University Press.

Buss, D. (1999). *Evolutionary Psychology*. Needham Heights, MA: Allyn & Bacon.

Buss, D. and Barnes, M. (1986). Preferences in human mate selection. *Journal of Personality and Social Psychology* **50**: 559–570.

Buss, D., Larsen, R.J., Westen, D. and Semmelroth, J. (1992). Sex differences in jealousy. *Psychological Science* **3**: 251–255.

Byrne, R. (1995). *The Thinking Ape*. Oxford: Oxford University Press.

Byrne, R.W. (1997). The technical intelligence hypothesis: an additional evolutionary stimulus to intelligence? In A. Whiten and R.W. Byrne (eds) *Machiavellian Intelligence II* (pp. 289–312). Cambridge, UK: Cambridge University Press.

Cartwright, J. (2000). *Evolution and Human Behaviour: Darwinian Perspectives on Human Nature*. London: Macmillan.

Chagnon, N. (1968). *Yanomamo:The Fierce People*. New York: Rinehart & Winston.

Chapman, T. (1997). The epidemiology of fears and phobias. In G.C.L. Davey (eds) *Phobias* (pp. 415–425). Chichester: Wiley.

Clutton-Brock, T.H. and Vincent, A.C.J. (1991). Sexual selection and the potential reproductive rates of males and females. *Nature* **351**: 58–60.

Crawford, C. (1998). Environment and adaptations: then and now. In C. Crawford and D.L. Kiebs (eds) *Handbook of Evolutionary Psychology*. Mahwah, NJ: Lawrence Erlbaum Associates Inc.

Cronin, H. (1991). *The Ant and the Peacock*. Cambridge, UK: Cambridge University Press.

Crook, J.H. and Crook, S.J. (1988). Tibetan polyandry. In L. Betzig, Borgehoff-Mulder and P. Turke (eds) *Human Reproductive Behaviour*. Cambridge, UK: Cambridge University Press.

Daly, M. (1997). Introduction. In G.R. Bock and G. Cardew (eds) *Characterising Human Psychological Adaptations* (pp. 1–4). Chichester: Wiley.

Daly, M. and Wilson, M. (1988). *Homicide*. Belmont, CA: Wadsworth.

Darwin, C. (1859). *On the Origin of Species by Natural Selection*. London: John Murray.

Dawkins, R. (1998). *Unweaving the Rainbow*. London: Penguin.

de Cantazaro, D. (1995). Reproductive status, family interactions, and suicidal ideation: surveys of the general public and high risk group. *Ethology and Sociobiology* **16**: 385–394.

Deacon, T.W. (1992). The human brain. In S. Jones, R. Martin and D. Pilbeam (eds) *The Cambridge Encyclopedia of Human Evolution* (pp. 115–122). Cambridge, UK: Cambridge University Press.

Deacon, T. (1997). *The Symbolic Species*. London: Penguin.

Delprato, D.J. (1989). Hereditary determinants of fears and phobias: a critical review. *Behaviour Therapy* **11**: 79–103.

Dennett, D. (1995). *Darwin's Dangerous Idea*. New York: Simon & Schuster.

Diamond, J. (1991). *The Rise and Fall of the Third Chimpanzee*. London: Vintage.

Diamond, J. (1997). *Why Sex is Fun: The Evolution of Human Sexuality*. London: Weidenfeld & Nicolson.

Dunbar, R. (1993). Co-evolution of neocortical size, group size and language in humans. *Behavioural and Brain Sciences* **16**: 681–735.

Dunbar, R. (1995). Are you lonesome tonight? *New Scientist* **145**(1964): 12–16.

Dunbar, R. (1996). *Grooming, Gossip and the Evolution of Language*. London: Faber & Faber.

Eibl-Eibesfeldt, I. (1989). *Human Ethology*. Hawthorne, NY: Aldine de Gruyter.

Einon, D. (1998). How many children can one man have? *Evolution and Human Behaviour* **19**: 413–426.

Ekman, P. (1973). *Darwin and Facial Expression: A Century of Research in Review*. New York: Academic Press.

Foley, R. (1987). *Another Unique Species*. Harlow: Longman.

Foley, R.A. (1989). The evolution of hominid social behavior. In V. Standen and R.A. Foley (eds) *Comparative Socioecology*. Oxford: Blackwell Scientific.

Fisher, A.E. (1962). Effects of stimulus variation on sexual satiation in the male rat. *Journal of Comparative Physiological Psychology* **55**: 614–620.

Garber, P.A. (1989). Role of spatial memory in primate foraging patterns: *Saguinus mystax* and *Saguinus fuscicollis*. American Journal of Primatology 19: 203–216.

Goodenough, J., McGuire, B. and Wallace, R. (1993). *Perspectives on Animal Behaviour*. New York: Wiley.

Gould, R.G. (2000). How many children could Moulay Ismail have had? *Evolution and Human Behaviour* **21**(4): 295.

Greenlees, I.A. and McGrew, W.C. (1994). Sex and age differences in preferences and tactics of mate attraction: analysis of published advertisements. *Ethology and Sociobiology* **15**: 59–72.

Guttentag, M. and Secord, P. (1983). *Too Many Women?* Beverly Hills, CA: Sage.

Hamilton, W.D. (1964). The genetical evolution of social behaviour, I and II. *Journal of Theoretical Biology* **7**: 1–52.

Harcourt, A.H. (1991). Sperm competition and the evolution of non-fertilizing sperm in mammals. *Evolution* **45**(2): 314–328.

Harcourt, A.H., Harvey, P.H., Larson, S.G. *et al.* (1981) Testis weight, body weight and breeding systems in primates. *Nature* 293: 55–57.

Harvey, P.H. and Bradbury, J.W. (1991). Sexual selection. In J.R. Krebs and W.B. Davies (eds) *Behavioural Ecology* (pp. 203–234). Oxford: Blackwell Scientific.

Hill, K. and Hurtado, M. (1996). *Demographic/Life History of Ache Foragers*. Hawthorne, NY: Aldine de Gruyter.

Hill, K. and Kaplan, H. (1988). Tradeoffs in male and female reproductive strategies among the Ache. In L. Betzig, M. Borgehoff-Mulder and P. Turke (eds) *Human Reproductive Behaviour*. Cambridge, UK: Cambridge University Press.

Holloway, R. (1999). Evolution of the human brain. In A. Lock and C.R. Peters (eds) *Handbook of Human Symbolic Evolution*. (pp. 74–126). Malden, MA: Blackwell.

Hosken, F.P. (1979). *The Hosken Report: Genital and Sexual Mutilation of Females*. Lexicon, MA: Women's International Network News.

Jerison, H.J. (1973). *Evolution of Brain and Intelligence*. New York: Academic Press.

Jones, S. (1991). We are all cousins under the skin. *The Independent* (London) 14.

Kirkpatrick, D.R. (1984). Age, gender, and patterns of common intense fears among adults. *Behaviour Research and Therapy* **22**: 141–150.

Kuch, K., Cox, B.J., Evans, R.E. and Shulman, I. (1994). Phobias, panic and pain in 55 survivors of road vehicle accidents. *Journal of Anxiety Disorders* **8**: 181–187.

Kvarnemo, C. and Ahnesjo, I. (1996). The dynamics of operational sex ratios and competition for mates. *Trends in Ecology and Evolution* **11**: 4–7.

Langlois, J.H. and Roggman, L.A. (1990). Attractive faces are only average. *Psychological Science* **1**: 115–121.

Littlefield, C.H. and Rushton, J.P. (1986). When a child dies: the sociology of bereavement. *Journal of Personality and Social Psychology* **51**(4): 797–802.

Lumsden, L.J. and Wilson, E.O. (1982). Precis of genes, mind and culture. *Behavioural and Brain Sciences* **5**: 1–7.

MacLean, P.D. (1972). Cerebral evolution and emotional processes: new findings on the striatal complex. *Annals of the New York Academy of Sciences* **193**: 137–149.

McGuire, M., Troisi, A. and Raleigh, M.M. (1997). Depression in an evolutionary context. In S. Baron-Cohen (ed.) *The Maladapted Mind*. Hove, UK: Psychology Press.

Miller, G. (1996). Sexual selection in human evolution. In C. Crawford and D.L. Krebs (eds) *Evolution and Human Behaviour*. Mahwah, NJ: Lawrence Erlbaum Associates Inc.

Miller, G.F. (1998). How mate choice shaped human nature: a review of sexual selection and human evolution. In C. Crawford and D.L. Krebs (eds) *Handbook of Evolutionary Psychology*. Mahwah, NJ: Lawrence Erlbaum Associates Inc.

Miller, G. (2000). *The Mating Mind*. London: Heinemann/Doubleday.

Milton, K. (1988). Foraging behaviour and the evolution of primate intelligence. In R.W. Byrne and A. Whiten (eds) *Machiavellian Intelligence*. Oxford: Oxford University Press.

Moore, H.D.M., Martin, M. and Birkhead, T.R. (1999). No evidence for killer sperm or other selective interactions between human spermatozoa in ejaculates of different males in vitro. *Proceeedings of the Royal Society of London Series B* **266**(1436): 2343–2350.

Murphy, D. and Stich, S. (2000). Darwin in the madhouse. In P. Caruthers and A. Chamberlain (eds) *Evolution and the Human Mind*. Cambridge, UK: Cambridge University Press.

Murray, C. and Lopez, A. (1996). Evidence-based health policy-lessons from the global burden of disease study. *Science* **274**: 740–743.

Nesse, M. and Williams, C. (1995). *Evolution and Healing: The New Science of Darwinian Medicine*. London: Weidenfeld & Nicolson.

Oakley, K. (1959). *Man the Toll-Maker*. Chicago: University of Chicago Press.

Parker, S. (1976). The precultural basis of the incest taboo: towards a biosocial theory. *American Anthropologist* **78**: 285–305.

Perrett, D.I., Burt, D.M., Penton-Voak, I.S., Lee, K.J., Rowland, D.A. and Edwards, R. (1999). Symmetry and human facial attractiveness. *Evolution and Human Behaviour* **20**: 295–307.

Price, L.H. (1968). The genetics of depressive behaviour. In A. Coppen and S. Walk (eds) *Recent Developments in Affective Disorders*. British Journal of Psychiatry Special Publication No. 2.

Ridley, M. (1993). *The Red Queen*. London: Viking.

Seligman, M.E.P. (1971). Phobias and preparedness. *Behaviour Therapy* **2**: 307–320.

Short, R.V. (1994). Why sex. In R.V. Short and E. Balaban (eds) *The Differences between the Sexes* (pp. 3–22). Cambridge, UK: Cambridge University Press.

Smith, E.A. and Bliege Bird, R.L. (2000). Turtle hunting and tombstone opening: public generosity as costly signalling. *Evolution and Human Behaviour* (21): 245–261.

Smith, P.K. (1979). The ontogeny of fear in children. In W. Sluckin (ed.) *Fear in Animals and Man*. London: Van Nostrand.

Smith, R.L. (1984). Human sperm competition. In R.L. Smith (ed.) *Sperm Competition and the Evolution of Animal Mating Systems*. Orlando, FL: Academic Press.

Smoller, J.W. and Tsuang, M.T. (1998). Panic and phobic anxiety: defining phenotypes for genetic studies. *American Journal of Psychiatry* **155**(9): 1152–1162.

Stevens, A. and Price, J. (1996). *Evolutionary Psychiatry*. London: Routledge.

Strachan, T. and Read, A.P. (1996). *Human Molecular Genetics*. Oxford: Bios Scientific.

Strassmann, B.I. and Dunbar, R.I.M. (1999). Human evolution and disease: putting the Stone Age in perspective. In S.C. Stearns (ed.) *Evolution in Health and Disease* (pp. 91–101). Oxford: Oxford University Press.

Symons, D. (1979). *The Evolution of Human Sexuality*. Oxford: Oxford University Press.

Symons, D. (1992). On the use and misuse of Darwinism. In J.H. Barkow, L. Cosmides and J. Tooby (eds) *The Adapted Mind* (pp. 137–159). Oxford: Oxford University Press.

Thornhill, R. and Gangestad, S.W. (1994). Human fluctuating asymmetry and sexual behaviour. *Psychological Science* **5**: 297–302.

Tomarken, A.J., Mineka, S. and Cook, M. (1989). Fear-relevant selective associations and covariation bias. *Journal of Abnormal Psychology* **98**: 381–394.

Tomasello, M. and Call, J. (1997). *Primate Cognition*. Oxford: Oxford University Press.

Trivers, R. (1972). Parental investment and sexual selection. In B. Campbell (ed.) *Sexual Selection and the Descent of Man*. Chicago: Aldine de Gruyter.

Warner, H., Martin, D.E. and Keeling, M.E. (1974) Electroejaculation of the great apes. *Annals of Biomedical Engineering* **2**: 419–432.

Weizmann, F., Wiener, N.I. and Wiesenthal, D.L. (1990). Differential K theory and racial hierarchies. *Canadian Psychology* **31**: 1–13.

Whiten, A. and Byrne, R. (1988). Tactical deception in primates. *Behavioural and Brain Sciences* **11**: 233–244.

Wirtz, P. (1997). Sperm selection by females. *Trends in Ecology and Evolution* **12**: 172–173.

Wynn, T. (1988). Tools and the evolution of human intelligence. In R.W. Byrne and A. Whiten (eds) *Machiavellian Intelligence*. Oxford: Oxford University Press.

Index

Page numbers of Glossary definitions are given in bold

Ache, 21, 35
Acrophobia, 79
Adaptation, 3, 6 , **169** *see also*
    environment of evolutionary
    adaptation (EAA)
Adaptive conservatism hypothesis,
    94–95
Adaptive significance, 6, **169**; of
    emotions, 69; and genetic
    disorders, 109, 111; and mate
    choice, 58; *see also* function
Adultery, 16, 56, 67, 69
Agoraphobia, 79
Alleles, 10, **169**; recessive, 10; *see
    also* genes, DNA, genome,
    chromosomes
Allometry, 125, **169**
Altruism, reciprocal, 88
Amino acids, 110
Anaemia, sickle-cell, 110
Anxiety, 76, 81, 82, 99
Apis mellifera, 103
Archetypes, 75
Asexual reproduction, 15
Attachment, 101

Australopithecines, 121, 128, 145,
    148, **169**
Australopithecus afarensis, 122,
    148
Australopithecus africanus, 122
Autism, 88, 108

Baboons, 143
Baron-Cohen, S., 88
Beauty, 30, 42
Bee, honey, 103
Behaviourism, 101, 135, **170**
Betzig, L., 22, 26
Bipedalism, 91, 124
Bipolar depression, 105, 106, 108,
    109
Bowlby, J., 101–2
Brain, 124, 125; growth of 127–129;
    metabolic demands of, 143; and
    sexual selection, 144; and tools,
    147
Breast-feeding, 23
Buss, D., 57, 61, 65, 79, 86
Byrne, R., 135, 142

Carriers, 10, **170** *see also* cystic fibrosis
Cartwright, J., 26
Catanzaro, D., 103
Chaperoning, 66
Childbirth, 91; risks of, 124
Chimpanzees, 51, 70, 90, 123, 128, 129, 143
Chromosomes, 110, **170** *see also* DNA, genes
Claustrophobia, 79
Clitoridectomy, 66
Coefficient of relatedness, 103, 106, **170** *see also* inclusive fitness
Common chimp *see* chimpanzees
Coolidge effect, 39
Costly signalling theory, 44–45
Crawford, C., 90
Cosmides, L., 76
Cystic fibrosis, 10, 111, **170**

Daly, M., 80
Damselfly, 40
Darwin, C., 1, 5, 28, 119; wheel of life, 4
Darwinism, 9
Dawkins, R., 145–146
Deacon, T., 130
Deception, 142; tactical in primates, 136 *see also* machiavellian intelligence
Delprato, D.J., 97
Dennett, D., 2
Depression, 105
Descent of Man, *28*, 119
Developmental theories, 100
Diabetes, 107
Disability-adjusted life years (DALYs), 93–94
Dishonest signals, 44, 46, **170**
Divorce, 67–68
DNA, 2, 110, 113, **170** *see also* genes, chromosomes
DSM, 86, 105
Dunbar, R., 92, 140

Ekman, P., 73–74
Elephant seals, 37
Emotions, 73–74
Encephalization, 127, 130; quotients, 128–129, 137, 139, 147
Endogenous depression, 105
Environment of evolutionary adaptation (EEA), 6, 76, 89, 90, 92, 97, 131, **170**
Evolutionary psychiatry, 113

Faces: attractiveness of, 62; baby, 62
Fears, 73, 77, 95
Fisher, R.A., 42
Fitness, 5, 7, **170** *see also* inclusive fitness
Foraging, 134
Freud, S., 9, 75, 89
Function, 82, 100, **170** *see also* ultimate cause; adaptive significance
Functional explanation, 8

Galton, F., and facial averageness, 63
Gametes, 15, 34, **171**
Gene pool, 18, **171**
Genes, 4, 12, 104, 109–111, **171** *see also* allele, good sense (genes), DNA, chromosomes
Genital mutilation, 66
Genome, 2, **171** *see also* genes, allele, DNA
Genotype, 12, **171**; contrast with phenotype, 4, 12 *see also* genome, allele, DNA
Genus, **171**
Good sense (genes) school, 42–44, **171**
Good taste school, 42–44
Gorilla gorilla, see gorillas
Gorillas, 53, 70, 129, 143
Group size, 112
Group-splitting hypothesis, 111,
Grouse, 30

Haemoglobin, 110
Hair, loss of, 123
Haldane, J., 103
Hamilton, W., 102–103 *see also* inclusive fitness
Harems, 22
Heritability, 107
Hinde, R., 101
Hominids, 3, 120, **171**
Homo erectus, 121, 122, 128, 148
Homo habilis, 121, 122, 123, 128
Homo sapiens, 2, 52, 91, 121
Honest signalling, 46, **171**
Howler monkeys, 138
Hummingbird, 29
Hunter-gathering, 21, 91
Huxley, T.H., 119

Immune system, 40, 64, **171**
Inbreeding, 11, **171**; and Westermarck effect, 9
Incest, 9
Inclusive fitness, 102, **171**
Infanticide, 80, **172**
Intelligence, 137
Intensionality, 135, **172**
Intrasexual competition, 34
Ismail the Bloodthirsty, 32

James, W., 1, 18
Jealousy, 64, 70
Jerison, H.J., 126
Jung, C.G., 89

Kamikaze sperm hypothesis, 41–42 *see also* sperm competition
Kazcynski, T., 88
Kibbutz, 11

Lactation, 19
Larynx, 146
Lineage, 131, **172** *see also* phylogeny
Lorenz, K., 101
Lumsden, L., 96

Machiavellian intelligence, 134, **172**

Machiavelli, N., 135
Maclean, P., 139
Major depressive disorder (MDD), 105
Malaria, 111
Mania, 105
Mate choice, 58; and advertisements, 60–61; data on preferences, 58
Mating: strategies, 25; systems, 20, 53
Mechanisms, 8
Mental disorders, 85
Miller, G., 144
Milton, K., 139
Mirounga angustrirostris, 37
Modularity, 75
Monogamy, 16, 19, 25, 70, **172**
Moore's law, 145
Mouse lemur, 125
Munch, E., 78, 81
Murphy, D., 86
Mutations, 3, **173**

Natural selection, 3 *see also* sexual selection
Neocortex, 139; volume of, 140–141
Neolithic revolution, 91–92
Normal distribution theory, 99

Oakley, K., 147
Oedipus complex, 11
Oestrus, 51, 54
Old Stone Age, 6, 37
Ontogenetic theories, 100
Operational sex ratio, **172**
Orang-utan, 52, 129, 143
Order, **172**
Origin of Species (On the), 1, 119
Ovulation, 23, 32–33,125, **172**
Ovum, 15

Pan troglodytes see chimpanzees
Paradigm, 2, 28, **172**
Parasites, 38, 44, 64, **172**

Parental investment, 30–31, **172**
Paternity confidence, 65
Pavlovian conditioning, 95
Peacock (*Pavo cristatus*), 27–28
Phenotype, 4, 5, 12, **173**
Phobias, 77, 95, 97–98
Pleiotropy, 110
Polyandry, 17, 25, **172**; among Tre-ba, 24
Polygamy, 17, 70, **172**
Polygynandry, 18
Polygyny, 16, 25, **172**
Pongo pygmaeus see Orang-utan,
Preparedness theory, 95
Price, J., 75, 111
Price, L.H., 105
Primate intelligence, 133–136
Promiscuity, 18, 66
Proximate causes, **173** *compare with* ultimate explanations
Proximate explanations, 7–8, 13

Rank theory of depression, 100
Reactive depression, 105
Relative risk, 107
Reproductive fitness, 5

Schizophrenia, 105–107
Seals, 37
Selection, **173** *see also* sexual selection, natural selection
Seligman, M.E.P., 95,
Sexual dimorphism, 28, 37, 49, 55, **173**; in body size, 49, 53, 70
Sexual reproduction, 15
Sexual selection, 27, 36, **173**; and brains, 144; intersexual selection, 30, 47; intra sexual selection, 29, 47
Sickle-cell anaemia, 110
Signals, 44, 46, 48
Singh, D., 167

Skinner, B. F., 135
Snakes, 96
Social homeostasis theory, 100
Sociobiology, 1
Sparthura underwoodi, 29
Species, 2, **173**
Sperm competition, 30, 40, 47, 52, **173**
Spider monkeys, 138
Spiders, 97.
Stevens, A., 75, 111
Stich, S., 86, 87
Strassman, B., 92
Strategy, 16, **173** *see also* game theory
Suicide, 104
Symmetry, 64, **173**
Systems (mating), 16

Taxonomy, **173**; of humans, 120
Testes, 50, 54, 70, **174**; significance of size, 51, 53, 54
Theory of mind, 134, **174**
Tooby, J., 76
Tools, 146–148
Trait, 6
Triune model of brain, 140
Trivers, R., 31
Turtle hunting, 46
Twins, 105

Ultimate explanations, 7–8, 13, **174**
Unipolar depression, 105

Waist to Hip ratio (WHR), 167
Watson, J.B., 101
Westermarck effect, 9–11 *see also* incest
Wilson, E.O., 96
Wilson, M., 80
Whitten, A., 135, 142
Wynn, T., 149